A Sentence a Day

Short, playful proofreading exercises
to help students avoid tripping up when they write

Samantha Prust

COTTONWOOD PRESS
A Prufrock Press Company
Please visit our website at http://www.prufrock.com

Cottonwood, a Prufrock Press Company
P.O. Box 8813
Waco, TX 76714-8813
Phone: (800) 998-2208
Fax: (800) 240-0333
http://www.prufrock.com

COTTONWOODPRESS

Introduction

Many teachers have adopted the daily proofreading exercises published by large companies as a way to help students practice finding and correcting errors. Sadly, many students have fallen asleep over these same exercises. I believe that these exercises try to do too much—i.e., force-feed facts and information as they also try to teach writing.

A Sentence a Day takes a different approach. It focuses on short, playful, interesting sentences with a sense of humor. Students receive proofreading practice in daily doses that don't overwhelm. Each exercise should take only a few minutes of class time, allowing for frequent, consistent reinforcement and practice of serious writing skills.

Make transparencies of the exercises for your own classroom use, or simply write each exercise on the board. Either way, I hope you will find that these exercises hold your students' attention much better than the standard fare.

—Samantha Prust

List of topics addressed on the page

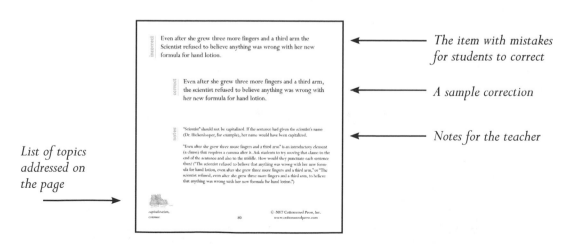

The item with mistakes for students to correct

A sample correction

Notes for the teacher

About the Author

Samantha Prust is a freelance writer who has contributed materials for many language arts textbooks. She has a master of fine arts degree in creative writing from Colorado State University.

The students found it very hard to believe that Mrs Snodwhumple had ever been a teenager herself, in fact they found it hard to believe that she was human at all.

The students found it very hard to believe that Mrs. Snodwhumple had ever been a teenager herself. In fact, they found it hard to believe that she was human at all.

"Mrs." requires a period.

The item is a run-on sentence. A period or a semicolon should be placed after "herself."

Introductory phrases like "by the way, "on the other hand," and "in fact" should be set off with commas.

A Sentence a Day

abbreviations, run-ons,
commas

The envelope enveloping the leter.

The envelope enveloping the letter was covered with pink hearts and red lipstick kisses.

The item is a sentence fragment. What *about* the envelope enveloping the letter?

Try having students complete the sentence in at least two more ways—adding something before the fragment (*Bart cautiously opened the envelope enveloping the letter*) and after the fragment (*The envelope enveloping the letter was covered with pink hearts and red lipstick kisses*).

For more practice, and some fun, challenge students to complete the fragment with other requirements as well—such as using the word "fear," including both a boy and a girl in the sentence, or adding a dog. Possibilities are endless.

"Letter" has two *t*'s.

fragments, spelling

No

6

A Sentence a Day

The nieghbors supposebly had a pet dodo bird that excaped but I no that dodo birds are extinct.

The neighbors supposedly had a pet dodo bird that escaped, but I know that dodo birds are extinct.

"Neighbors" is one of those aggravating words that does *not* follow the "*i* before *e* except after *c*" rule.

Despite how some people pronounce the word, there is no *b* in "supposedly." Similarly, there is no *x* in "escaped."

"Know" is the word needed, not "no."

The sentence is a compound sentence (two complete sentences connected with "and," "but," "or," "for," "nor," and sometimes "yet" and "so.") Therefore, it needs a comma.

A Sentence a Day

9-6

spelling, word choice, commas

incorrect

The star athlete turned out to be a alien. From the newly discov-ered planet gezbarkawda.

correct

The star athlete turned out to be an alien from the newly discovered planet Gezbarkawda.

notes

Students often create sentence fragments by putting in a period too soon. The two fragments above are easily fixed by simply removing the period.

"A" is used before words beginning with a consonant sound. "An" is used before words beginning with a vowel sound. (For some reason, the use of "a" instead of "an" seems to be increasing. It might be interesting to speculate with students as to *why*.)

Because "Gezbarkawda" is the name of a specific planet, it should be capitalized—even if it is fictional.

fragments, word choice,
capitalization

9–10

A Sentence a Day

My brother, Sundar, he puts catsup and maple syrup on everything.

My brother Sundar puts catsup and maple syrup on everything.

People often use double subjects, especially when they are talking informally. Examples: *My mother, she won't let me go camping with my boyfriend for three weeks in Alaska. My boyfriend, he thinks she's being unreasonable. My dad, he won't even let me talk to him about it.* However, these double subjects are completely unnecessary and actually kind of silly. *My mother won't let me go camping* is simpler and just as clear as *My mother, she won't let me go camping.*

Appositives interrupt a sentence to give more information about a noun in the sentence. Usually they are set off with commas. However, a one-word appositive such as "Sundar" doesn't really need commas.

double subjects,
commas

A Sentence a Day

9-12

9

It is supposebly difficult to pat your head rub your stomach and chew gum at the same time.

It is supposedly difficult to pat your head, rub your stomach(,) and chew gum at the same time.

Although many people pronounce the word "supposebly" (with a *b*), the word is really "supposedly" (with a *d*).

Words in a series should be separated by commas. However, the final comma (the serial comma) is really optional, unless its elimination creates confusion in meaning. Interestingly, magazine and newspaper publishers tend to leave it out, following the *Associated Press Stylebook*. Book publishers are more likely to rely on the *Chicago Manual of Style*, which recommends leaving it in. Students are often amazed to find out that authorities can differ on punctuation rules.

spelling,
commas

NO

A Sentence a Day

Who's idea was it to allow students to ride skateboards in the hall.

Whose idea was it to allow students to ride skateboards in the hall?

Any sentence that asks a question should have a question mark at the end.

"Who's" is a contraction of "who is." A test: try substituting "who is" in the sentence to see if it makes sense. If it does, use "who's." If it doesn't, use "whose."

A Sentence a Day

9-14

question marks,
word choice

A even-toed ungulate which is better known as a camel keeps the sand out of it's eyes with 3 eyelids.

An even-toed ungulate, which is better known as a camel, keeps the sand out of its eyes with three eyelids.

"An" is used before words beginning with a vowel sound.

"Which is better known as a camel" is an appositive. It interrupts the flow of the sentence to give more information about "ungulate" and should be set off with commas.

"Its" is a pronoun used to show ownership or possession. There is no apostrophe in it.

Numbers smaller than ten are generally spelled out, not written as numerals. Therefore, "3" should be written as "three."

word choice, commas
miscellaneous

A Sentence a Day

After Lee took a break to walk his Iguana and pet his Python he went back to work on his marshmellow sculpture.

After Lee took a break to walk his iguana and pet his python, he went back to work on his marshmallow sculpture.

"After Lee took a break to walk his iguana and pet his python" is an introductory element (a clause). Therefore, it should be followed by a comma.

"Iguana" is a kind of lizard, just as "python" is a kind of snake. However, they aren't the names of *specific* iguanas or pythons. If the iguana's name is "Ethel," "Ethel" is what should be capitalized, not "iguana."

"Marshmallow" is the correct spelling.

A Sentence a Day

commas, capitalization, spelling

Sept 18

The mall closed it's doors lifted into the air and flew off into space with a large and handsome truck stop.

The mall closed its doors, lifted into the air(,) and flew off into space with a large and handsome truck stop.

Never mind that the mall in this sentence is behaving in a decidedly peculiar fashion. It is doing three things, and those three things should be separated by commas. The final comma in a series is considered optional.

"It's" is a contraction of "it is." A test: substitute "it is" in the sentence to see if "it's" is what is needed. If it doesn't sound right, "its" should be used.

commas,
word choice

A Sentence a Day

Pleeze do not sneeze, or wheeze near there cheeze.

Please do not sneeze or wheeze near their cheese.

Annoying as it may be that all these words with an "eez" sound aren't spelled alike at the end, they are not.

Should it be "there," "they're," or "their"? "Their" is the word used to show possession.   It is "their" cheese someone should not be sneezing or wheezing near.

spelling,
word choice

A Sentence a Day

Sept 20

As Lionel was finally doing his laundry after letting it sit, in a heap for two weeks. He watched in horror as a mustard splotch on one of his shirts, unstuck itself and crawled out of the laundry basket, and down the hall.

As Lionel was finally doing his laundry after letting it sit in a heap for two weeks, he watched in horror as a mustard splotch on one of his shirts unstuck itself and crawled out of the laundry basket and down the hall.

Students commonly create sentence fragments simply by inserting a period too soon. Read aloud the first "sentence" so that students hear how it is left hanging and needs to be completed.

All the commas in the incorrect version are unnecessary. (An argument can be made for including one before "in a heap" for emphasis. In that case, a comma is necessary after "heap" as well.)

Some grammarians would point out that splitting the verb "was doing" with the word "finally" is not a good idea. They might leave out the word "finally" altogether or write, "As Lionel was doing his laundry, finally, he…" Others would leave the "finally" where it is.

*fragments,
commas*

16

A Sentence a Day

"I looked over the close in my closet and decided I'm going to wear to scarfs around my neck and one on my head, to," said Tiffany. "Is that *all* your going to where?" gasped her mother.

"I looked over the clothes in my closet and decided I'm going to wear two scarves around my neck and one on my head, too," said Tiffany.

"Is that *all* you're going to wear?" gasped her mother.

The corrected sentences use "to, two, and too" correctly.

"Clothes" refers to what you wear. "Close" is what you do to a door.

"Wear" is what you do with clothes. "Where" is used to refer to a place.

In dialogue, a new paragraph begins with each change of speakers.

A Sentence a Day

17

word choice,
dialogue

incorrect

The eye-catching float adorned with silver and yellow balloons. Carried a gigantic ice sculpture of a earthworm, the high schools mascot.

correct

The eye-catching float adorned with silver and yellow balloons carried a gigantic ice sculpture of an earthworm, the high school's mascot.

notes

The two sentence fragments above can be turned into a complete sentence simply by removing the period.

Since "earthworm" begins with a vowel sound, the phrase should be "an earthworm."

The mascot "belongs" to the high school. Therefore, an apostrophe is needed before the *s*.

fragments, word choice, apostrophes

A Sentence a Day

Sept 26

A skunk wandered through the neighbor hood and caused quit a scene when it ambled over to the busstop and crawled up on the bench.

A skunk wandered through the neighborhood and caused quite a scene when it ambled over to the bus stop and crawled up on the bench.

"Neighborhood" is one word.

"Bus stop" is two words.

"Quite" is the word needed above, not "quit," which means to give up.

A Sentence a Day

Sept 28

spelling,
word choice

Iris ate icecream on the ice berg while the yak yakked about frozen Yogurt.

Iris ate ice cream on the iceberg while the yak yakked about frozen yogurt.

"Ice cream" is two words.

"Iceberg" is one word.

There is no need to capitalize "yogurt."

spelling,
capitalization Oct 2

A Sentence a Day

The scarred moose vamoosed disapearing behind the caboose.

The scared moose vamoosed, disappearing behind the caboose.

Some students may insist that the moose really was *scarred* in an accident, not *scared*. They could be right, though it is more likely that the moose is disappearing because it is scared, not because it is scarred. However, allow their argument. It's good for them to see that small things like an *r* can completely change the meaning of a sentence.

"Disappearing," however, definitely does need two *p*'s.

"Disappearing behind the caboose" is an ending element (a phrase) that interrupts the flow of the sentence. It should be preceded by a comma.

A Sentence a Day

*spelling,
commas*

incorrect

"Before you buy shoes for your pet millipede", he said. "Consider the cost.

correct

"Before you buy shoes for your pet millipede," he said, "consider the cost."

notes

Commas go *inside* (before) closing quotation marks.

If a quotation is interrupted with a dialogue tag ("he said," "she said," etc.), the next part of the quotation should not be capitalized unless it starts a new sentence. "Before you buy shoes for your pet millipede, consider the cost" is a complete sentence interrupted with "he said." Therefore, "consider" is not capitalized.

Quotation marks always come in pairs. One set is always followed by another.

Bram had a hard time remembering things, he always came to school with a sticky note list stuck in the middle of his fourhead.

Bram had a hard time remembering things. He always came to school with a sticky note list stuck in the middle of his forehead.

The important thing to note in the incorrect item above is that it is a run-on sentence (or comma splice). A comma alone cannot separate two sentences. An interesting exercise is to have students see how many ways they can fix the run-on. A few ways:

- Because Bram had a hard time remembering things, he always came to school with a sticky note list stuck in the middle of his forehead.

- Bram had a hard time remembering things. That's why he always came to school with a sticky note list stuck in the middle of his forehead.

- Bram always came to school with a sticky note list stuck in the middle of his forehead because he had a hard time remembering things.

"Forehead" is the correct spelling.

A Sentence a Day

run-ons,
spelling

Aisha asked the telemarketer, "if she could call him back tomorow around dinnertime at his home phone number."

Aisha asked the telemarketer if she could call him back tomorrow around dinnertime at his home phone number.

Quotation marks can be compared to a "bubble" in a cartoon strip. The bubble shows the words coming out of the cartoon character's mouth. Similarly, quotation marks surround only the words a character actually says. The incorrect item above is an indirect quote. It tells what Aisha asked, but without using her exact words. The sentence could also be corrected this way: Aisha asked the telemarketer, "May I call you back tomorrow around dinnertime at your home phone number?"

"Tomorrow" has two *r*'s.

Incidentally, Aisha's technique for dealing with telemarketers can be very satisfying.

quotation marks,
spelling

A Sentence a Day

Oliver was upset this morning, because his little brother fed his homework to squeezy there pet Boa Constrictor.

Oliver was upset this morning because his little brother fed his homework to Squeezy, their pet boa constrictor.

"Because" is a conjunction that is not generally preceded by a comma. (The conjunctions that *are* generally preceded by a comma when they separate two sentences are "and," "but," "or," "for," "nor," and sometimes "yet" and "so.")

"Squeezy" is the name of a specific boa constrictor. Therefore, it is a proper noun that should be capitalized. "Boa constrictor" is the name of a type of snake, but it is not the name of a specific, individual snake. Therefore, it is *not* capitalized.

"Their" is used to show possession. It was "their" boa constrictor; it belonged to them.

A Sentence a Day

commas, capitalization, word choice

Irregardless of what I thought of the movie I definitely enjoyed the gigantic bucket of buttered popcorn that me and my friend shared.

Regardless of what I thought of the movie, I definitely enjoyed the gigantic bucket of buttered popcorn that my friend and I shared.

Some would say that "irregardless" is not really a word, just as "ain't" is not. However, both clearly *are* words, since people use them all the time. However, they are considered "nonstandard." They should not be used in most writing or speaking.

"Me and my friend" is increasingly showing up everywhere. "My friend and I" is the correct form. An interesting point of discussion is *why* "me and my friend" is becoming so common. Some say it might have to do with a growing self-centeredness in our society. That "me first" attitude seeps into language as well as behavior. It's something to think about, in any case, and could lead to an interesting discussion. (The item is not written as a direct quotation. If it had been, "me and my friend" could remain in order to record the person's words accurately.)

word choice,
pronouns

A Sentence a Day

Dont slam the door, you will wake up the penguins.

Don't slam the door because you will wake up the penguins.

"Don't" needs an apostrophe. As in all contractions, the apostrophe takes the place of the letter or letters left out in the contraction. (In this case, it stands for the *o* in "not.")

The item is a run-on sentence. A comma, alone, cannot separate two sentences.

A Sentence a Day   Ott4

apostrophes,
run-ons

Adriana knew something was wrong when she seen a giraffe poke it's head out of her chimney.

Adriana knew something was wrong when she saw a giraffe poke its head out of her chimney.

"Seen" always needs a helping verb before it—she *has* seen, she *will have* seen, she *was* seen, she *will be* seen, etc. Unfortunately, "she seen" is so common that it sounds right to some students.

"It's" is a contraction of "it is." "Its" (without the apostrophe) is always used to show possession of some kind (its fur, its wheels, its stomach, its head, etc.).

verb form,
word choice

A Sentence a Day

In the alley behind the restraunt Margo was cornered by a gang of fried chickens who demanded that she put down her coleslaw and mashed potatos and come out with her hands up.

In the alley behind the restaurant, Margo was cornered by a gang of fried chickens who demanded that she put down her coleslaw and mashed potatoes and come out with her hands up.

The introductory prepositional phrases ("in the alley behind the restaurant") should be followed by a comma. They precede the main part of the sentence: "Margo was cornered by a gang of fried chickens."

The word "potato" does not end in an *e*. An *e* is added, however, when the word is made plural. (Students may be interested to hear the story about former Vice President Dan Quayle's famous gaffe regarding the word. When visiting a school, he corrected a student who had spelled potato correctly, without an *e*. Quayle told him that "potato" had an *e* on it—and was the butt of jokes for a very long time.)

A Sentence a Day Oct 9

commas,

spelling

Instead of ringing the phone made a sound like boots squishing thru mud.

Instead of ringing, the phone made a sound like boots squishing through mud.

"Instead of ringing" is an introductory phrase. (It comes before the main part of the sentence: "the phone made a sound like boots squishing through mud.") Therefore, it should be followed by a comma.

You might want to talk about the increasing use of "thru" in advertising, instant messages, text messages, and many e-mail messages. The proper spelling is still "through," but it is very likely that one day "thru" will be accepted as normal. Students need to know that language rules *do* change. For example, "skyscraper" used to be considered a slang word. Now it is actually the proper name for very tall buildings.

commas,
spelling

A Sentence a Day

To get alot of attention put on a carrot costume and walk around on a pair of expecially high stilts.

To get a lot of attention, put on a carrot costume and walk around on a pair of especially high stilts.

"A lot" is two words, not one. No one writes "alittle." Why write "alot"? It doesn't make sense.

"To get a lot of attention" is an introductory element (a phrase) that should be followed by a comma.

People often mispronounce "especially" as "expecially"—which leads them to spell the word incorrectly as well. There is no *x* in "especially."

A Sentence a Day

Oct 12

spelling, commas

Elizabeth didn't ever take all the attention she got from James and Sam and Delmar for granite, and she kept all the boy's hundreds of letters in a special file cabinet in her closet.

Elizabeth didn't ever take all the attention she got from James and Sam and Delmar for granted, and she kept all the boys' hundreds of letters in a special file cabinet in her closet.

"Granted" is the word needed, not "granite," which is a kind of rock.

In most cases, the apostrophe goes after the *s* if the possessive refers to more than one person. In this case it does. (An example of when it would not: Jodie shopped in the women's department.) If it referred to only one boy's letters, the apostrophe would go before the *s*.

word choice,
apostrophes

A Sentence a Day

The banana split that I ate last night at humongo ice cream shoppe, sat in my stomache like a ball of hardened clay.

The banana split that I ate last night at Humongo Ice Cream Shoppe sat in my stomach like a ball of hardened clay.

There is no need for the comma before "sat."

Humongo Ice Cream Shoppe is the name of a store, so it should be capitalized.

"Shoppe" is part of the store's name, so the spelling should remain. Many retail establishments use the spelling "shoppe" to give their stores an old-fashioned flavor. (Whether their technique is effective or not is another question.)

A Sentence a Day

commas, capitalization,
miscellaneous

I crept along the hallway to surprise Mom with a boquet of flours, I also wanted to shock my sister with the digital photo I took of her kissing her boyfriend when she was suppose to be studing at the libary.

I crept along the hallway to surprise Mom with a bouquet of flowers. I also wanted to shock my sister with the digital photo I took of her kissing her boyfriend when she was supposed to be studying at the library.

It takes an eagle eye to catch all the little (and big!) things wrong with this sentence. "Bouquet" and "flowers" are the correct spellings of Mom's surprise.

The sentence is a run-on. The comma after "flours" should be replaced with a period or a semicolon. An alternative would be to leave the comma and add "and."

Even though it sounds like "suppose to" when we say it, the correct spelling is "supposed to."

"Studying" is what the sister was supposed to be doing at the library.

spelling, run-ons

A Sentence a Day

Our nieghbor poured cool gray concrete over his entire yard cuz he didnt want to water the grass anymore.

Our neighbor poured cool gray concrete over his entire yard because he didn't want to water the grass anymore.

This item is a sea of misspelled words. "Neighbor" is, unfortunately, one of those words that breaks the "*i* before *e* except after *c*" rule.

The word is "because," not "cuz." "Cuz" is an abbreviation used only in the most informal writing among friends.

"Didn't" needs an apostrophe. The word is a contraction of "did" and "not," and the apostrophe is used in place of the missing *o*.

A Sentence a Day

spelling, apostrophes

My best freind sally, she says you should always wash your elbows before going out 2 eat.

My best friend Sally says you should always wash your elbows before going out to eat.

"Friend" is very commonly misspelled as "freind." The word does follow the "*i* before *e* except after *c*" rule.

There is no reason to say "my best friend Sally" *and* "she." The sentence needs only one subject.

Using "2" instead of "to" may be acceptable in text messages to friends, but it should not be used in other kinds of writing.

spelling,
double subjects

A Sentence a Day

I should of bought the robot, it would of cleaned my room, taken out the trash, and done my homework.

I should have bought the robot. It would have cleaned my room, taken out the trash(,) and done my homework.

When we speak, the contractions "should've" and "would've" sound like "should of" and "would of." The "of" should be "have," however. (The item could also be written like this: I should've bought the robot. It would've cleaned my room, taken out the trash, and done my homework.)

Two complete sentences cannot be separated by a comma. They require a comma and a coordinating conjunction ("and," "but," "or," "for," "nor," "yet," "so"), a semicolon, or a period between them.

word choice,
run-ons

A Sentence a Day

Oct 19

"Your such a know-it-all" said the Heart, to the Brain.

"You're such a know-it-all," said the heart to the brain.

"You're" is a contraction of "you are" and is the word needed in this sentence.

The quotation should be separated from "said the heart to the brain" with a comma.

There is no need for a comma after "heart."

There is no need to capitalize "heart" and "brain."

word choice, commas,
capitalization

A Sentence a Day

"Your overly sensitive", said the brain. To the heart.

"You're overly sensitive," said the brain to the heart.

This short item has a lot wrong with it. First, "your" should be "you're." "You're" is a contraction of "you are."

The comma should go inside (before) the closing quotation marks. Except in very rare cases, the comma *always* goes inside the quotation marks.

Finally, "To the heart" is a sentence fragment. It is really part of the previous sentence.

A Sentence a Day

word choice, commas,
fragments

Her and me are gonna go shoping for a Collie puppy and a yo-yo.

She and I are going to go shopping for a collie puppy and a yo-yo.

Ask students what they would say if only one person were going shopping. Would they say, "Her is going shopping"? "Me is going shopping"? Of course not. Then why say "her and me"?

"Gonna" should be "going to."

"Shopping" needs two *p*'s. It is common to double the final consonant before adding "ing."

"Collie" is the name of a kind of dog. However, it is not the name of a specific dog, like "Sophie" or "Spot." Therefore, it should not be capitalized.

pronouns, spelling, capitalization

A Sentence a Day

"Alright, I'll do it" sighed the dragon. "I'am not going to like it, but I'll stop breatheing fire on the village."

"All right, I'll do it," sighed the dragon. "I'm not going to like it, but I'll stop breathing fire on the village."

"All right" is two words.

"All right, I'll do it" should be set off from "sighed the dragon" with a comma.

"I'am" is a common misspelling, even though it doesn't make much sense. An apostrophe in a contraction stands for a letter left out, but in "I'am," nothing is left out. "I'm" is the correct spelling.

"Breathe" has an *e* at the end. "Breathing" does not. In most cases, the final *e* is dropped before adding "ing" to a word that ends in *e*.

If you've got to have a dragon, it's nice to at least have an agreeable one.

A Sentence a Day

*spelling,
commas*

He held out his hands to catch the football, then he glanced at Kiyoko to see if she was chearing for him, when he turned back, the football hit him right in the face.

He held out his hands to catch the football and then glanced at Kiyoko to see if she was cheering for him. When he turned back, the football hit him right in the face.

"Cheering" is the correct spelling.

The item is one long run-on sentence. You might have students experiment to see how many ways they can rewrite the sentence, correcting it and keeping the same meaning. Two examples:

After holding out his hands to catch the football, he glanced at Kiyoko to see if she was cheering for him. When he turned back, the football hit him right in the face.

He held out his hands to catch the football. He glanced at Kiyoko to see if she was cheering for him. He turned back. The football hit him right in the face.

spelling,
run-ons

A Sentence a Day

"You hafta let me go mom," whined Keisha. "I want to see the singing burro"!

"You have to let me go, Mom," whined Keisha. "I want to see the singing burro!"

"Hafta" should be "have to."

Because "Mom" is what Keisha calls her mother, it is a name that should be capitalized.

Because Keisha is directly addressing her mother, "Mom" should be set off with commas.

The exclamation point belongs inside the quotation marks since it applies to the sentence, "I want to see the singing burro!"

A Sentence a Day   Oct 25   43

spelling, capitalization, commas, exclamation points

After the tiny baby bird opened it's tiny beak, and let out an earsplitting squawk that made my sister drop her Slurpee. I laughed.

After the tiny baby bird opened its tiny beak and let out an ear splitting squawk that made my sister drop her Slurpee, I laughed.

"Its" (with no apostrophe) is the word needed to show possession. (The beak "belongs" to the baby bird.)

The item is really one sentence. "I laughed" is the main part of the sentence (the independent clause). "After the tiny baby bird opened its tiny beak and let out an earsplitting squawk that made my sister drop her Slurpee" is a very long introductory element (a subordinate clause).

word choice,
fragments

A Sentence a Day

I ain't gonna be no candy cane in no school play!

I'm not going to be a candy cane in any school play!

The incorrect version of this sentence has a certain flavor missing in the correct version. You might want to see if students have any ideas why the correction is less satisfying than the original.

"Ain't" is indeed a word. It is used all the time. However, it is considered "non-standard" usage and should be avoided in most circumstances.

"Gonna" should be "going to."

A very old guideline in English is to avoid double negatives. Since the sentence starts out early on with a "not," the "no's" should be omitted.

A Sentence a Day

word choice, spelling
double negatives

Then the career counselor goes, "we have alot of job openings for accountants that are abominable snowmen.

Then the career counselor said, "We have a lot of job openings for accountants who are abominable snowmen."

The career counselor didn't "go." She "said." Informally, people use "go" instead of "said" a lot, but it's better to avoid it, especially in writing.

"A lot" is two words.

The first word in a sentence should be capitalized. The first word in the sentence the career counselor is saying should therefore be capitalized.

Quotation marks always come in pairs. They should appear at the beginning *and* the end of the quotation.

"Who" is for people. "That" is for things.

word choice, spelling,
capitalization, quotation marks

A Sentence a Day

I never before new a gnu, said the new zoo worker.

"I never before knew a gnu," said the new zoo worker.

"New" is used for things that are not old. "Knew" is used for things you understand or are acquainted with.

Quotation marks go around the exact words that someone speaks.

A Sentence a Day ○ Ct 3D 47

word choice,
quotation marks

There is a word for every thing, including the pale area shaped like a half-moon at the base of a finger nail, it's a *lunule*.

There is a word for everything, including the pale area shaped like a half-moon at the base of a fingernail. It's a *lunule*.

"Everything" is one word. So is "fingernail."

The incorrect item is a run-on sentence. A comma cannot be used, by itself, to separate two sentences. A period, a semicolon, or a comma with a coordinating conjunction ("and," "but," "or," "for," "nor," "yet," "so") should be used to separate the sentences.

spelling,
run-ons

A Sentence a Day

Carmen my friend who loves music even more than chocolate had a iPod surgically inplanted in her brain.

Carmen, my friend who loves music even more than chocolate, had an iPod surgically implanted in her brain.

"My friend who loves music even more than chocolate" is an appositive that gives more information about the noun, Carmen. It interrupts the flow of the sentence and should be set off with commas.

What do you do with the word "iPod"? It's annoying to have a brand name that does *not* follow the rules about capitalizing proper nouns. In this case, the company has chosen to write the name of a product with a lowercase *i*. Therefore, that's the way we should write it, too. (The exception would be if "iPod" comes at the beginning of the sentence. Then it should be capitalized.)

Because it begins with a vowel sound, it should be "an iPod," not "a iPod."

The word is "implanted," not "inplanted."

A Sentence a Day

commas, capitalization, word choice, spelling

If I had one wish. I would wish that I had a milion more wishes.

If I had one wish, I would wish that I had a million more wishes.

"If I had one wish" is a sentence fragment. Replacing the period with a comma easily fixes it, making "If I had one wish" an introductory clause.

"Million" is the correct spelling.

fragments,
spelling

A Sentence a Day

Be careful not to mispell your name on the entry form for the Spelling Bee.

Be careful not to misspell your name on the entry form for the spelling bee.

"Misspell" is, sadly, often misspelled. Note that the letter *s* appears twice.

There is no need to capitalize "spelling bee," just as there is no need to capitalize "the track meet" or "the club meeting." If the official name were mentioned, the name *would* be capitalized. (Example: Roberts County Annual Spelling Bee.)

spelling,
capitalization

A Sentence a Day   Nov 1

The affects of my sun burn—peeling itching blistered skin and a lot of pain—effected my ability to attend the annual beach BBQ.

The effects of my sunburn—peeling, itching, blistered skin (,) and a lot of pain—affected my ability to attend the annual beach barbecue.

Students have to be really on their toes for this one. "Effects" is a noun. "Affects" is a verb. Therefore, the sentence should read, "The effects of my sunburn..." and "...affected my ability to attend...."

"Peeling, itching, blistered skin, and a lot of pain" is a series that requires commas.

"Sunburn" is one word.

"BBQ" is fine for informal e-mail or text messages. However, for most other situations, the word should be spelled out as "barbecue" or "barbeque."

word choice, commas,
spelling

A Sentence a Day

Who says men are'nt nurturing, a male Emperor Penguin protects his egg for sixty days or more, and doesn't eat during the time he is waiting for the egg to hatch.

Who says men aren't nurturing? A male emperor penguin protects his egg for sixty days or more and doesn't eat during the time he is waiting for the egg to hatch.

The item above has a host of problems. First of all, it is a run-on sentence. "Who says men aren't nurturing?" is a question and should have a question mark.

The apostrophe is in the wrong place in "aren't."

The term "emperor penguin" describes a kind of penguin. It should not be capitalized. (If we were talking about a penguin named Frank, "Frank" *would* be capitalized.)

In most cases, a comma is not needed between the subject and the predicate of a sentence. There is no need for a comma after "more."

A Sentence a Day

run-ons, apostrophes
capitalization, commas

The principle's principle principal is, "Treat others the way you want to be treated.

The principal's principal principle is, "Treat others the way you want to be treated."

"Principal" and "principle" are easily confused. When referring to a person, "principal" is the word. (Think, "The princiPAL is my PAL.") "Principal" is also used to mean "main, first, or foremost in importance," as in "the principal focus of the meeting." "Principle" is used to refer to a rule or standard.

If students point out that the sentence is confusing even when the words are spelled correctly, great. It is. Have them suggest ways to improve it, as in, "The principal has one main rule for students to remember: Treat others the way you want to be treated."

The sentence should end with quotation marks, as quotation marks come in pairs.

word choice,
quotation marks

A Sentence a Day

Between you and I, I'm glad the cats' stole the fish sticks.

Between you and me, I'm glad the cats stole the fish sticks.

Though many believe "between you and I" is correct, it is not. The phrase requires the objective case of the pronoun—"me." (If you don't want to try to explain this to kids having a hard time just recognizing a complete sentence, no one will blame you.)

Something you definitely *should* note is the superfluous apostrophe in "cats." After they start studying apostrophes, students all too often start sprinkling them everywhere, even where they are not needed.

A Sentence a Day

pronouns, apostrophes

All of the sudden the Loch Ness Monster decided to come out of the water and open a Chuck E. Cheese franchise.

All of a sudden, the Loch Ness monster decided to come out of the water and open a Chuck E. Cheese franchise.

For some unknown reason, people have begun saying "all of *the* sudden" instead of "all of *a* sudden." Why? Who knows? The conventional phrase, and the one that should appear in written works, is "all of a sudden."

"Loch" is capitalized because it is the name of a lake (Lake Ness). There is no reason to capitalize "monster."

"All of a sudden" is an introductory element (a phrase) that should be followed by a comma.

word choice, capitalization,
commas

Nov 5

56

A Sentence a Day

Maria ceretainly can throw that javellin good.

Maria certainly can throw that javelin well.

"Well" is used to describe how someone *does* something. "Good" is used to describe a noun. Examples:

He coached them well.
He was a good coach.
She cooks well.
She is a good cook.

Have students come up with other examples of "good" and "well" being used correctly.

"Certainly" and "javelin" are the correct spellings.

A Sentence a Day

Nov 7

word choice,
spelling

These ones are diferent from those ones.

These are different from those.

An oddity that has crept into our language is the use of "these ones." There is no need for the "ones." Why not just say "these"? Or "those"?

"Different" has two *f*'s.

unnecessary words, spelling

A Sentence a Day

I ain't got no problem attending english class but I wish the teacher would stop talking to us about using good grammer. I don't want no part of learning how to speak good.

I don't have any problem attending English class, but I wish the teacher would stop talking to us about using good grammar. I don't want any part of learning how to speak well.

One thing to point out about the word "ain't" is how often it is used by writers to help suggest that a character is uneducated or not very bright. "Ain't" users can, of course, be both educated *and* bright, but others may not always perceive them that way.

"I ain't got no" is a double negative—another no-no (pun intended!).

"English" is capitalized because it is the name of a language.

"Grammar" is spelled "gramm*ar*," not "gramm*er*." Many people are surprised to learn that.

"Well" is used to describe how someone *does* something. "Good" is used to describe a noun. (It was a *good* concert. She sang *well*.)

A Sentence a Day

word choice, double negatives, capitalization, spelling

My Mom, went to the store too buy some bread!!!!! And I ate it!!!!!

My mom went to the store to buy some bread, and I ate it.

"Mom," "Dad," "Grandma," "Grandpa," etc., are not capitalized when they are preceded by a pronoun such as "your" or "my." However, if "Mom" is used as a person's name, it is capitalized. (Example: I looked around and saw Mom.)

"To" is the word to use, not "too." "Too" is used to express a degree of something, as in "too much ice cream." "Too" can also be used to mean "also."

Exclamation points should be used *very* sparingly. They should be reserved for the truly amazing. Eating bread doesn't qualify.

capitalization, word choice, miscellaneous

A Sentence a Day

Richard didn't understand why he didn't get the job at the Insurance company. After all he was friendly in his interview. He winked at the secretary and called the President "dude."

Richard didn't understand why he didn't get the job at the insurance company. After all, he was friendly in his interview. He winked at the secretary and called the president "dude."

No capital letter is needed for "insurance company" since the name of the insurance company isn't used.

"After all" is an introductory expression like "on the other hand" or "nevertheless." Therefore, it needs a comma.

In most cases, "president" is not capitalized unless it is used with the president's name, as in "President Kennedy." Many textbooks teach that "President" should be capitalized when it is used to refer to the president of the United States, whether it is used with his name or not. However, many other references take the opposite approach—for example, the *Associated Press Stylebook* and the *Chicago Manual of Style*.

A Sentence a Day

capitalization,
commas

The narly not on the old tree, looked like a nome's nuckle.

The gnarly knot on the old tree looked like a gnome's knuckle.

Students may have trouble figuring out what the item above means. If they do, it's a good opportunity to point out why spelling matters. The item includes words that use "gn" and "kn" for the "n" sound.

There is no need for the comma in the sentence.

spelling, commas

A Sentence a Day

Because the meatball rolled off the table on to the floor and out the door yesterday at noon in the cafeteria.

Because the meatball rolled off the table, onto the floor(,) and out the door yesterday at noon in the cafeteria, I didn't get any protein for lunch.

Sentence fragments are not necessarily short. The fragment above is an example of a fairly long one. It needs to be completed. However, you might first have students see if they can make the fragment even longer, while keeping it a fragment. For example, they might write, "Because the meatball rolled off the table, onto the floor, and out the door yesterday at lunchtime in the cafeteria during the third lunch period at Hamilton Junior High in the center of South Dakota." That long introductory element (a clause) would still be a fragment.

Items in a series need to be separated by commas. The last comma is optional.

A Sentence a Day

fragments,
commas

Over the course of six weeks we learned how to lasso a Groundhog, and throw a elegant holiday dinner party for eight.

Over the course of six weeks, we learned how to lasso a groundhog and throw an elegant holiday dinner party for eight.

"Over the course of six weeks" is an introductory element consisting of two prepositional phrases. It should be followed by a comma.

There is no need to capitalize "groundhog," just as there is no need to capitalize "cat" or "dog" or "scissors" or "car."

"An" is used before words that begin with a vowel sound.

There is no need for a comma after "groundhog."

commas, capitalization,
word choice

Nov 9

A Sentence a Day

when pennsylvania state university honored ralph for his dedication to studing insects, he was thrilled and celebrated by giving cake crumbs to all the bugs in his lab.

When Pennsylvania State University honored Ralph for his dedication to studying insects, he was thrilled and celebrated by giving cake crumbs to all the bugs in his lab.

Names of specific schools are always capitalized, as are names of people.

"Studying" is a word that is often misspelled. The *y* is important.

A Sentence a Day

Nov 13

capitalization, spelling

My dad couldn't decide weather or not to let me borrow his car again, even though I done it last week and didn't have any problems except for crashing into the tour bus outside the Museum.

My dad couldn't decide whether or not to let me borrow his car again, even though I did it last week and didn't have any problems, except for crashing into the tour bus outside the museum.

"Weather" refers to rain, sunny skies, snow, hurricanes, etc. "Whether" is the word needed for "whether or not."

"I done" is always incorrect. "Done" needs a helping verb. ("I *have* done," "I *will have* done," "We *are* done," for example.) "I did" is correct in the sentence above.

"Museum" should not be capitalized unless it is part of the name of the museum, as in "Metropolitan Museum of Art."

word choice, verb form,
capitalization

Nov 15

A Sentence a Day

Fern felt kinda funny after the all-you-can-eat octopus buffet the one held every friday night at Fish R Us.

Fern felt kind of funny after the all-you-can-eat octopus buffet, the one held every Friday night at Fish R Us.

"Kinda" may be okay for very informal e-mails between friends. In other cases, it should be spelled "kind of."

The sentence ends with an appositive, "the one held every Friday night at Fish R Us." It interrupts the sentence to give us more information about the buffet. It should be preceded by a comma.

Days of the week are capitalized.

"Fish R Us" is an unfortunate name for a restaurant, and that *R* instead of "Are" is annoying. However, if a restaurant chooses to spell its name incorrectly, we have to live with it.

A Sentence a Day

spelling, commas, capitalization

Mr. washburns old car would'nt be able to win a race against a Cheetah, which can run as fast as 70 miles per hour. Niether would Mr. washburn.

Mr. Washburn's old car wouldn't be able to win a race against a cheetah, which can run as fast as 70 miles per hour. Neither would Mr. Washburn.

"Washburn's" must be capitalized because it is a name. It also needs an apostrophe to show possession.

The apostrophe in "wouldn't" is in the wrong place.

"Cheetah" does not need to be capitalized, as it doesn't name a specific cheetah.

"Neither" is another exception to the "*i* before *e* except after *c*" rule.

capitalization, apostrophes, spelling

A Sentence a Day

I was like too tired to like wash the dishes and vacume and like do the rest of the chores my mom told me she would like me to do, so I went to the mall and like walked around and stuff with my friends.

I was too tired to wash the dishes and vacuum and do the rest of the chores my mom told me she would like me to do, so I went to the mall and walked around and talked with my friends.

The only "like" necessary in the item above is the one in "she would *like* me to do." The others are just fillers common in informal speech today.

"Vacuum" surprises many with its two *u*'s. There is no *e* at the end.

What does "and stuff" mean? A person should write what he or she means by "and stuff."

A Sentence a Day

Nov 19

unnecessary words, spelling, word choice

Jeremy kinda sorta liked playing football, baking cheesecake, ect.

Jeremy kind of liked playing football and baking cheese-cake.

"Kinda" and "sorta" stand for "kind of" and "sort of." Either "kind of" or "sort of" should be used here, not both phrases.

"Etc." is spelled with the *t* first—something that surprises many people, particularly those who incorrectly pronounce the word as "*eck* cetera."

"Etc." stands for "and so forth" and is used when the reader can guess what the "and so forth" might stand for. It generally follows a list of at least three items, so that a person can determine a pattern. What on earth can the "etc." stand for after "playing football, baking cheesecake"? The kind of sentence where "etc." *would* be appropriate is this one: Jeremy kind of liked playing football, soccer, basketball, etc. There we can detect a pattern—that Jeremy likes active sports.

spelling, unnecessary words, miscellaneous

A Sentence a Day

Even a busted clock, is right twice a day.

Even a broken clock is right twice a day.

"Broken" should be used instead of "busted" for all but the most informal conversation among friends.

There is no need to place a comma between the subject and the verb of a sentence.

word choice,
commas

A Sentence a Day

Nov 21

Only one mammel can fly with out the help of technology, the bat.

Only one mammal can fly without the help of technology: the bat.

"Mammal" ends in "al," not "el."

"Without" is one word, not two.

The sentence makes an announcement, a "Ta-da!" kind of announcement that means, "Note what follows." A colon or a dash is appropriate in such a sentence. A comma is not.

spelling,
colons

A Sentence a Day

"I'm not picky" Argued Aiden. "I'm particular. Nothing I eat on thursday can be green.

"I'm not picky," argued Aiden. "I'm particular. Nothing I eat on Thursday can be green."

A punctuation mark must separate a quotation from a dialogue tag like "argued Aiden." Generally, that punctuation mark is a comma, though sometimes an exclamation point or question mark is appropriate.

"Thursday" is a proper noun that must begin with a capital letter.

Quotation marks come in pairs. They belong at the beginning *and* at the end of a quotation. The item above lacks one at the end.

A Sentence a Day

punctuation, capitalization, quotation marks

At the present time dan is training grass hoppers to jump over hurdles, he hopes he can sell them someday to a Circus.

Dan is training grasshoppers to jump over hurdles. He hopes he can sell them someday to a circus.

"At the present time" isn't really wrong. However, there is no need for these rather formal sounding words—particularly in a sentence about grasshoppers—when the words "is training" already indicate that he is doing it at the present time, i.e., "now."

Dan is someone's name, so it should be capitalized.

Dan may be hoping to sell the grasshoppers to a circus, but he doesn't name which one. Therefore, "circus" should not be capitalized.

"Grasshoppers" is one word, not two.

Finally, the item is a run-on sentence. A comma cannot be used to separate two sentences.

unnecessary words, capitalization,
spelling, run-ons

A Sentence a Day

Talitha likes puppys and stuff.

Talitha likes puppies, kittens, bunnies, and other cute baby animals.

"Puppies" is the correct spelling.

"And stuff" is not clear. We can only guess what Talitha likes. Does she like walking puppies? Playing with them? Toilet training them? Does she like puppies and all other animals? "And stuff" needs clarification.

spelling, miscellaneous

all of the sudden captain skelly exclaimed weve been hit. were sinking. I want my mommy.

All of a sudden, Captain Skelly exclaimed, "We've been hit! We're sinking! I want my mommy!"

The correct phrase is "all of *a* sudden."

"Captain Skelly" is a proper name and should be capitalized.

Since the captain is exclaiming (with good reason), his words should have exclamation points after them. His words also need to be enclosed with quotation marks.

"We've" and "we're" need apostrophes. "We've" stands for "we have," and "we're" stands for "we are."

word choice, capitalization, exclamation
points, quotation marks, apostrophes

Nov 29

A Sentence a Day

When mr. martinez saw keith at the mall after school, he goes, "didn't you tell me you had to fly to your great grandmother's funeral today"? "Why weren't you in class"?

When Mr. Martinez saw Keith at the mall after school, he said, "Didn't you tell me you had to fly to your great grandmother's funeral today? Why weren't you in class?"

"Mr. Martinez" and "Keith" should be capitalized because they are names. "Didn't" should be capitalized because it is the first word in the sentence that Mr. Martinez speaks.

Mr. Martinez "said." He didn't "go."

Quotations marks go at the beginning of a quotation and at the end, not around each sentence in the quotation.

When the sentence being quoted is a question, the question mark goes *before* the quotation marks.

A Sentence a Day

capitalization, word choice, quotation marks

"Shannon please bring in the accordions ukuleles and kazoos" said the Music teacher.

"Shannon, please bring in the accordions, ukuleles(,) and kazoos," said the music teacher.

When a person is being directly addressed, his or her name is set off with a comma. Have students try putting Shannon's name in different parts of the sentence. ("Please bring in the accordions, ukuleles, and kazoos, Shannon," or "Please bring in the accordions, Shannon, and also the ukuleles and kazoos.")

No capital is needed for "music." School subjects are *not* capitalized unless they are languages or the names of specific sections, such as "Music 101."

Items in a series should be separated by commas. The final comma is considered optional.

A comma must separate the direct quotation from the dialogue tag, "said the music teacher."

commas,
capitalization

A Sentence a Day

Searching for Chuck our pet chinchilla we looked everywhere even in the toilet Chuck liked to do the backstroke and in the refrigerator vegetable drawer Chuck liked to munch on radishes

Searching for Chuck, our pet chinchilla, we looked everywhere, even in the toilet (Chuck liked to do the backstroke) and in the refrigerator vegetable drawer (Chuck liked to munch on radishes).

This is a proofreading item that will really challenge students. It introduces parenthetical information that should be enclosed in parentheses. (Some might choose dashes, which are also acceptable.) "Chuck liked to do the backstroke" and "Chuck liked to munch on radishes" are both asides that give more information. Because they are complete sentences, they must be separated from the main part of the sentence with something more than commas.

"Our pet chinchilla" is an appositive that interrupts the sentence to give more information about Chuck. It should be set off with commas.

A Sentence a Day

miscellaneous,
commas

Even after she grew three more fingers and a third arm the Scientist refused to believe anything was wrong with her new formula for hand lotion.

Even after she grew three more fingers and a third arm, the scientist refused to believe anything was wrong with her new formula for hand lotion.

"Scientist" should not be capitalized. If the sentence had given the scientist's name (Dr. Hickenlooper, for example), her name would have been capitalized.

"Even after she grew three more fingers and a third arm" is an introductory element (a clause) that requires a comma after it. Ask students to try moving that clause to the end of the sentence and also to the middle. How would they punctuate each sentence then? ("The scientist refused to believe that anything was wrong with her new form-ula for hand lotion, even after she grew three more fingers and a third arm," or "The scientist refused, even after she grew three more fingers and a third arm, to believe that anything was wrong with her new formula for hand lotion.")

capitalization,
commas

A Sentence a Day

Jake sat at his desk daydreaming and wondering, if squash could play squash, would they get squashed.

Jake sat at his desk daydreaming and wondering, "If squash could play squash, would they get squashed?"

Jake's thoughts should be treated as a quotation. He is speaking to himself, even if it is only in his thoughts. Therefore, quotations marks go around "If squash could play squash, would they get squashed?" Also, "If" is capitalized because it is the first word in the sentence being quoted.

Because the quotation is a question, it ends in a question mark. The question mark goes *before* the quotation marks, since the quotation itself is a question. If the sentence were a question, but the quotation itself were not, the question mark would go outside the quotation marks. (Example: Do you like it when the teacher says, "Stop talking and get busy"?)

A Sentence a Day

quotation marks, capitalization
question marks

Concerned about the fate of birds while the dragon was still lose. The Queen had all the birds in the Kingdom except magpies locked up in cages she didn't like magpies.

Concerned about the fate of birds while the dragon was still loose, the queen had all the birds in the kingdom except magpies locked up in cages. She didn't like magpies.

The first part of the item is a sentence fragment. The second is a run-on sentence.

"Lose" should be "loose." "Loose" rhymes with "caboose."

"The queen" and "kingdom" should not be capitalized since they are not specifically named.

This item is a good one for experimentation. Have students rewrite the sentence as many ways as possible, keeping the same meaning and recognizing that some versions will be better than others. (Example: Except for the magpies, which she didn't like, the queen was concerned about the fate of birds while the dragon was still loose. That is why she had all the birds in the kingdom locked up in cages.)

Renatta Reynaldo rested on the bed for a moment. Wishing she could change out of her beaded evening gown into jeans and a sweatshirt and go for a spin on her Harley Davidson Motorcycle.

Renatta Reynaldo rested on the bed for a moment, wishing she could change out of her beaded evening gown into jeans and a sweatshirt and go for a spin on her Harley Davidson motorcycle.

The item is really one sentence, not two. "Wishing she could change…and go for a spin on her Harley Davidson motorcycle" is really a dependent clause that should be part of the previous sentence.

"Harley Davidson" is capitalized because it is the brand name of the motorcycle. "Motorcycle" should not be capitalized.

A Sentence a Day

Dec 3

fragments,
capitalization

drive safe.

Drive safely.

The first word of a sentence should be capitalized.

"Drive" is a verb. "Safely" is an adverb. A verb needs an adverb to describe it. Therefore, the correct sentence is, "Drive safely." (Admittedly, people who insist on "Drive safely" are probably fighting a losing battle. "Drive safe" has become so common that it doesn't sound wrong to most people.)

"Safe" would be the word needed if you wanted to describe the *driver*, as in, "He was a a safe driver." Then "safe" would be an adjective.

capitalization,
word choice

A Sentence a Day

Well in my opinion pizza from pizza palooza makes a hole lot better snack than celery sticks and low-fat Cottage Cheese.

Well, in my opinion, pizza from Pizza Palooza makes a whole lot better snack than celery sticks and low-fat cottage cheese.

Introductory words like "yes," "no," "oh," and "well" are followed by a comma. The "well" doesn't really add anything to the sentence and could be eliminated. However, if it is included, it should have a comma after it.

"Pizza Palooza" is capitalized because it is the name of a restaurant. "Cottage cheese" should not be capitalized as it is not the name of a certain brand.

"In my opinion" is a parenthetical expression that should be set off with a comma.

A "hole" is something dug in the ground. "Whole" is the word needed here.

A Sentence a Day   Dec 5   85

Leafs fall in the Fall and leaf behind a blanket of red and orange covering the city streets every november. Well, maybe not in Antarctica.

Leaves fall in the fall and leave behind a blanket of red and orange covering the city streets every November…well, maybe not in Antarctica.

Many people are surprised that the seasons of the year are not capitalized. Months are capitalized; seasons are not.

The plural of "leaf" is "leaves." "Leave" is also a verb, as in "leave behind."

"Well, maybe not in Antarctica" is a sentence fragment. Rewriting it as, "Well, maybe this doesn't happen in Antarctica" is correct but seems to lack a little something—humor, perhaps?—that is implied in the original. Another solution is the one chosen above, to add ellipses and leave the fragment with the first sentence as an afterthought.

apitalization, spelling
ragments

A Sentence a Day

Mrs. Tahini asked "what was wrong with me?" when I came into class wearing only a giant garbage bag with a bike chain belt around the middle and kleenex boxes as shoes.

Mrs. Tahini asked what was wrong with me when I came into class wearing only a giant garbage bag with a bike chain belt around the middle and Kleenex boxes as shoes.

Because Mrs. Tahini's exact words are not used, quotation marks are not needed. Neither is a question mark. (She didn't say, "What was wrong with me?") The sentence could include a direct quotation if it were altered to read like this:

Mrs. Tahini asked, "What is wrong with you?" when I came into class wearing only a giant garbage bag with a bike chain belt around the middle and Kleenex boxes as shoes.

"Kleenex" is a brand name for tissues. Therefore, it should be capitalized.

A Sentence a Day

quotation marks,
capitalization

My favorite thing at the circus is: the clowns, the magicians, the daring young men and women on the flying trapeze and the deep-fried Twinkies.

My favorite things at the circus are the clowns, the magicians, the daring young men and women on the flying trapeze, and the deep-fried Twinkies.

The speaker is not listing a favorite thing. He or she is listing favorite *things*. The verb should also be changed to "are," to agree with "things."

A colon is not used with a list when the list immediately follows a verb. To use a colon, the part of the sentence before the colon should really be a sentence itself. Here is an example:

Here is a list of my favorite things at the circus: the clowns, the magicians, the daring young men and women on the flying trapeze, and the deep-fried Twinkies.

Although the last comma in a series is usually considered optional, this sentence is clearer *with* it.

verb agreement,
colons, commas

A Sentence a Day

I don't know why every one got so upset when I brought Harry my pet Tarantula to French Class and let him out of his cage to stretch his legs.

I don't know why everyone got so upset when I brought Harry, my pet tarantula, to French class and let him out of his cage to stretch his legs.

"Everyone" is one word, not two.

"My pet tarantula" is an appositive that interrupts the sentence to give more information about Harry. Therefore, it should be set off with commas.

"Harry" is capitalized because it is the tarantula's name, but "tarantula" should not be.

"French" is capitalized because it is made from the word "France." However, there is no reason to capitalize "class."

A Sentence a Day

spelling, commas, capitalization

Dec 11

After Mr. Fendlehessy gave detailed instructions for constructing a time machine Cecilia asked him to repeat them again.

After Mr. Fendlehessy gave detailed instructions for constructing a time machine, Cecilia asked him to repeat them.

"After Mr. Fendlehessy gave detailed instructions for constructing a time machine" is an introductory element (a clause). It should be followed by a comma.

There is no need to say "again." "Repeat" already means "say again." See if students can think of other examples of unnecessary words. (A few examples: "two twins," "7:00 p.m. in the evening," "advance planning.")

commas,
unnecessary words

A Sentence a Day

Drive East past the world's largest ball of twine, then take a left at highway 41 and go North until you reach The Farm where my Cousin lives with his pet Ostriches and 63 Turtles.

Drive east past the world's largest ball of twine. Then take a left at Highway 41 and go north until you reach the farm where my cousin lives with his pet ostriches and 63 turtles.

Directions of the compass (east, north) should not be capitalized.

A comma can't be used to separate two sentences. A period or a semicolon is needed after "twine."

There is no need to capitalize "the farm," "cousin," "ostriches," or "turtles." None of them are names of specific farms, cousins, ostriches, or turtles.

Street and road names like "Highway 41" should be capitalized.

A Sentence a Day

Dec 13

capitalization,
run-ons

No I don't like to eat at granola universe on green street, all it has on the menu is stuff like arugula and mushroom tarts and cabbage pudding.

No, I don't like to eat at Granola Universe on Green Street because all it has on the menu is food like arugula and mushroom tarts and cabbage pudding.

Introductory words like "yes," "no," "oh," and "well" should be followed by a comma.

Names of restaurants and specific streets should be capitalized.

Two sentences separated by only a comma form a run-on sentence. A period could be used after "Green Street." However, eliminating the comma and adding "because" also solves the problem.

Finally, the sentence could be improved by getting rid of the vague word "stuff."

commas, capitalization,
run-ons, word choice

A Sentence a Day

Carolines favorite Summer vacation spot is Osage beach in Ozarks state park near Kansas city, MO, but thats because of the cute life guard named Jonah that works there every year.

Caroline's favorite summer vacation spot is Osage Beach in Ozarks State Park near Kansas City, Missouri, but that's because of the cute lifeguard named Jonah who works there every year.

Because it is a possessive, "Caroline" should end in an apostrophe and an *s*.

Seasons of the year are not capitalized. Names of specific places are.

Generally, postal abbreviations of states should be confined to envelopes and lists. It's usually best to spell out the state when writing sentences.

"That's" is the correct spelling of the contraction for "that is."

"Lifeguard" is one word.

A person is a "who," not a "that."

A Sentence a Day

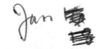

23

apostrophes, capitalization, abbreviations, spelling, word choice

Because there mother insisted they dress a like in pink dresses the twin girls always carried spare outfits in there jim bags and hurried into the restroom every morning to change.

Because their mother insisted they dress alike in pink dresses, the twin girls always carried spare outfits in their gym bags and hurried into the restroom every morning to change.

"Because their mother insisted they dress alike in pink dresses" is an introductory element (a clause) that should be set off with a comma.

"Their" is the word used whenever something or someone "belongs" to someone else. It is *"their"* mother." It is *"their"* gym bag.

"Alike" is one word.

"Gym" is the correct spelling for the kind of bags the girls carried.

commas, word choice, spelling Jan 18

94

A Sentence a Day

incorrect

"I know you don't beleive there's actualy a job position called "odor judge" said Thor "but there is, and I'am gonna apply for it first thing tommorow."

correct

"I know you don't believe there's actually a job position called 'odor judge,'" said Thor, "but there is, and I'm going to apply for it first thing tomorrow."

notes

"Believe" follows the "*i* before *e* except after *c*" rule.

"Actually" has two *l*'s. "Tomorrow" has two *r*'s but only one *m*.

"I am" does not need an apostrophe. "I'm" does. There is no such word as "I'am."

"Gonna" should be "going to."

The sentence is interrupted with "said Thor" in the middle, so "said Thor" should be set off with commas on each side.

The phrase "odor judge" should have single quotation marks around it since it occurs within a quotation with double quotation marks.

A Sentence a Day

95

Jan. 25

spelling, apostrophes, commas, quotation marks

I'm not commited to the commitee, because it requires to much committment.

I'm not committed to the committee because it requires too much commitment.

This item has some tricky spelling issues. "Committed" and "committee" each have double *t*'s. "Commitment," however, does not.

A common error is to place a comma before "because" when it occurs in the middle of a sentence (in this case, introducing a subordinate clause). No comma is needed.

"Too" is the word needed to express an amount or degree, as in "too much commitment."

spelling,
commas, word choice

A Sentence a Day

7th grade History teacher Mr. Meckelhenny has a nite job as drummer for the popular rock band, the hairy hecklers.

Seventh grade history teacher Mr. Meckelhenny has a night job as drummer for the popular rock band, the Hairy Hecklers.

When numbers occur as the first word in a sentence, they are spelled out.

School subjects are not capitalized, except for foreign languages. (Foreign languages are capitalized because they are formed from the names of countries.) Specific course titles such as "Introduction to Human Physiology 326" *are* capitalized.

"Night" is the correct spelling.

The band's name should be capitalized. (Students may argue that the real name of the band is "The Hairy Hecklers." That's a reasonable argument, though the usual practice is *not* to capitalize articles before the name of a group, as in "the Beatles," not "The Beatles."

A Sentence a Day

Jan 29

spelling, capitalization

Travel West on this road, it will eventually take you wear you want to go if wear you want to go is Podunk City.

Travel west on this road. It will eventually take you where you want to go, if where you want to go is Podunk City.

Directions are not capitalized. (If the sentence read, "I am going to travel to the West," it would be capitalized. Then "West" would refer to an area of the country, not a direction.)

A comma cannot be used alone to separate two sentences. A period or a semicolon should be added after "road." An even better option would be to eliminate choppiness by rewriting the sentence altogether, perhaps like this: If you travel west on this road, it will eventually take you where you want to go, if where you want to go is Podunk City.

The word is "where," not "wear." "Wear" is what you do with clothing.

The comma before "if" is not absolutely necessary, but it does make the sentence a bit clearer.

capitalization, run-ons,
word choice, commas

A Sentence a Day

Who has seen the building plans for that new building the one they named the trauma center for pampered cats.

Who has seen the building plans for that new building, the one they named the Trauma Center for Pampered Cats?

The sentence is a question, so it should end in a question mark.

The name of the new center should be capitalized.

"The one they named the Trauma Center for Pampered Cats" is an appositive that gives more information about the building. Therefore, it should be preceded by a comma.

A Sentence a Day

question marks,
capitalization, commas

Jeanette decided to find out for her self why Mr. Kantz never let jaws his pit bull out of the backyard. It was not a good decision.

Jeanette decided to find out for herself why Mr. Kantz never let Jaws, his pit bull, out of the backyard. It was not a good decision.

"Herself" is one word, not two.

"His pit bull" is an appositive that interrupts the sentence to give more information about "Jaws." Therefore, it should be set off with commas.

"Jaws" is the name of a specific pit bull. It should be capitalized.

Its not bad having a chef for a mom, except when she tries out recipes like the ones for: fudge-dipped mustard cookies or tangy vinegar milk shakes.

It's not bad having a chef for a mom, except when she tries out recipes like the ones for fudge-dipped mustard cookies or tangy vinegar milk shakes.

"It's" is the word needed when "It is" can be substituted in the sentence.

A colon is not necessary. It *would* be if the sentence read differently. "It's not bad having a chef for a mom, except when she tries out recipes like these: fudge-dipped mustard cookies or tangy vinegar milk shakes" is an example.

A Sentence a Day

word choice, colons

To punish his younger brother for telling on him and getting him in trouble on the Bus, Edward smeared Chunky Peanut Butter under his pillow dropped Happy Fish Tuna Surprise on the sheets and let in the Cat.

To punish his younger brother for telling on him and getting him in trouble on the bus, Edward smeared chunky peanut butter under his pillow, dropped Happy Fish Tuna Surprise on the sheets(,) and let in the cat.

Items in a series should be separated by commas. The comma before the "and" is optional.

There is a lot of unnecessary capitalization going on in the item. There is no need to capitalize "bus" or "chunky peanut butter." "Happy Fish Tuna Surprise" is the brand name of a specific product, so it is capitalized. There is no need to capitalize "cat."

Jared use to be a good student and a great soccer player, however now he is only a great soccer player.

Jared used to be a good student and a great soccer player. However, now he is only a great soccer player.

Students frequently substitute "use to" for "used to," probably because it sounds like "use to" when they say it. However, it is properly spelled "used to."

The item is a run-on sentence. A comma cannot separate two sentences. A period or a semicolon is needed between "player" and "however."

Introductory words like "however," "nevertheless," or "therefore" should be followed by a comma.

A Sentence a Day

spelling, run-ons, commas

Kareem felt such a loss when his pet hermit crab got lose and wandered out into the street and into the path of a Ford Truck.

Kareem felt such a loss when his pet hermit crab got loose and wandered out into the street and into the path of a Ford truck.

"Lose" and "loose" are often confused. "Loose" both rhymes with and looks similar to "goose."

"Ford" is capitalized because it is a brand name. "Truck" is not part of the name. If the grasshopper had encountered a Ford Taurus, "Taurus" would have been capitalized because it *is* part of the brand name of a particular automobile.

word choice,
capitalization

A Sentence a Day

"I don't know Rebecca where you think your going in that outfit," remarked her father, "but it certainly isn't out of this house."

"I don't know, Rebecca, where you think you're going in that outfit," remarked her father, "but it certainly isn't out of this house."

When a person is addressed, by name, the name is set off with commas.

"You're" should be used instead of "your" because "you're" is short for "you are."

There is no way to correct Rebecca's choice of clothing. Her father needs to do that.

A Sentence a Day

commas,
word choice

I like pizza, hamburgers, tostadas, and ice cream a hole lot better than the Organic green beans, tofu, lettuce, and figs that my Mom always brings home, my brother still talks about and not in a good way the broccoli butterscotch chip cookies she made once.

I like pizza, hamburgers, tostadas, and ice cream a whole lot better than the organic green beans, tofu, lettuce, and figs that my mom always brings home. My brother still talks about—and not in a good way—the broccoli butterscotch chip cookies she made once.

This item has a number of problems. First of all, "whole" is the word needed, not "hole." A "hole" is something in the ground or in a doughnut.

There is no reason to capitalize "organic" or "mom."

A period is needed after "home." Without it, the sentence is a run-on.

"And not in a good way" is a parenthetical aside that interrupts the sentence. Dashes are appropriate to set it off. Parentheses are also acceptable.

word choice, capitalization,
run-ons, punctuation

A Sentence a Day

The depressed dentist decided to stop flossing and treat himself to peanut brittle taffy licorish and caramel apples.

The depressed dentist decided to stop flossing and treat himself to peanut brittle, taffy, licorice(,) and caramel apples.

Commas are needed to separate items in a series.

"Licorice" is the correct spelling.

The dog and the cat was both sleeping on my backpack, so I couldn't possibly do my homework. That's why I never done it.

The dog and the cat were both sleeping on my backpack, so I couldn't possibly do my homework. That's why I never did it.

The first sentence has a plural subject, so it needs a plural verb—"were."

"Done" needs a helping verb with it, as in "I *have* not done my homework." With no helping verb, "did" is the word to use.

verb form,
verb tense

A Sentence a Day

Allison should of asked before she borrowed you're diamond earrings because I know you're gonna be mad. Especially when you find out she lost them.

Allison should have asked before she borrowed your diamond earrings because I know you're going to be mad, especially when you find out she lost them.

Although the phrase *sounds* like "should of," it's really spelled "should have."

"You're" is a contraction of "you are." It should only be used when you can substitute "you are" in the sentence and have it make sense—as in "I know *you are* going to be mad." "Your" is used to show possession, as in "*your* diamond earrings."

"Gonna" should be spelled "going to."

"Especially when you find out she lost them" is a fragment that belongs with the previous sentence.

A Sentence a Day

spelling, word choice, fragments

incorrect

When he got a big pimple on his nose on the opening night of the play that stared him as a handsome hunk that was suppose to have all the girls falling in love with him.

correct

When he got a big pimple on his nose on the opening night of the play that starred him as a handsome hunk who was supposed to have all the girls falling in love with him, Mario decided he didn't want to show up.

notes

Although it is very long, the item above is still a sentence fragment. It needs to be finished. What *happened* right after Mario got the big pimple on his nose?

Girls may have "stared" at Mario, but he "starred" in the play.

People are referred to as "who," not "that."

It may sound like "suppose to," but the phrase is correctly spelled "supposed to."

fragments, word choice, spelling

A Sentence a Day

Sipping Cokes and strolling along, a truck suddenly appeared ahead of us.

Sipping Cokes and strolling along, we saw a truck suddenly appear ahead of us.

"Sipping Cokes and strolling along" is a dangling modifier. It sounds as though the truck is sipping Cokes and strolling along. That's because an introductory phrase should apply to the first noun after it—in this case, "truck." The sentence needs to be rewritten.

A Sentence a Day

dangling
modifiers

incorrect

For all intensive purposes, Howard was really the teacher in the class, he new alot more than the real teacher.

correct

For all intents and purposes, Howard was really the teacher in the class. He knew a lot more than the real teacher.

notes

Many people mistakenly believe that the phrase is "for all intensive purposes." However, the phrase is really "for all intents and purposes."

A period or a semicolon is needed after "class." A comma alone cannot be used to separate two sentences.

"Knew" is the word needed, not "new."

"A lot" is two words, not one.

word choice,
run-ons, spelling

A Sentence a Day

"I'm running away to join the circus and become a clown," said Amelia. I realy hope the other clowns will except me, share there big rubber lips, give me tips on makeup, ect."

"I'm running away to join the circus and become a clown," said Amelia. "I really hope the other clowns will accept me, share their big rubber lips, give me tips on makeup, etc."

"Really" has two *l*'s.

"Except" means "all but this." "Accept" is the word needed here.

It should be "*their* big rubber lips." "Their" is used to show possession.

"Etc." is really pronounced "*et* cetera," not "*eck* cetera." It is spelled that way, too, with the *t* coming before the *c*.

Quotation marks are needed before "I," as quotation marks come in pairs.

A Sentence a Day

spelling, word choice, quotation marks

Jake's mother collects antiques and is looking for a mahogany desk suitable for a woman with thick legs and large drawers.

Jake's mother collects antiques and is looking for a mahogany desk with thick legs and large drawers, suitable for a woman.

The problem with this item is the placement of "with thick legs and large drawers." By placing the phrase after "woman," it sounds as though she is looking for a woman with thick legs and large drawers.

dangling modifiers

A Sentence a Day

Zachary ate a apple and a orange and then decided hed had enuff healthy food, he called perfect pizza palace and ordered a anchovy and pepperoni pizza with extra cheeze.

Zachary ate an apple and an orange and then decided he'd had enough healthy food. He called Perfect Pizza Palace and ordered an anchovy and pepperoni pizza with extra cheese.

"An" is used with words that begin with a vowel sound, such as "apple," "orange," and "anchovy."

"He'd" needs an apostrophe, since it is a contraction of "he had."

"Enough" doesn't have any *f*'s in it.

"Perfect Pizza Palace" is the name of a specific pizzeria, so it should be capitalized.

"Cheese" may sound like it has a *z* in it, but it doesn't.

The item is a run-on sentence. A comma can't be used to separate complete sentences.

A Sentence a Day

115

*word choice, apostrophes, spelling
capitalization, run-ons*

Calvin put down his money and signs up for the "Teenagers Who Don't Get an Allowance" bowling turnament.

Calvin put down his money and signed up for the "Teenagers Who Don't Get an Allowance" bowling tournament.

The item above switches tenses. It starts out with a verb in past tense ("put") and switches to present tense ("signs"). The sentence should be rewritten so that all the verbs are in past tense.

"Tournament" is the correct spelling.

It is not incorrect to remove the quotes around "Teenagers Who Don't Get an Allowance." It's the name of the tournament, but since it's a rather odd name, the quotation marks help distinguish it as a name. It is also possible that "bowling tournament" is part of the official name of the event. Therefore, "Teenagers Who Don't Get an Allowance Bowling Tournament" should also be considered correct.

verb tense, spelling

A Sentence a Day

The mischievious mannequins came to life when the department store closed, they changed out of their silk dresses into shorts and sweatshirts and playing baseball in the cosmetics department.

The mischievous mannequins came to life when the department store closed. They changed out of their silk dresses into shorts and sweatshirts and played baseball in the cosmetics department.

The item above is really two sentences. A comma cannot be used to separate two sentences.

"Mischievous" is often misspelled (and mispronounced) with an extra *i* after the *v*.

The second sentence has a problem in parallelism. The verbs are "changed" and "playing." "Playing" should be changed to "played" to match the form of the first verb and to help the whole thing make sense. (Ask students to read the incorrect version aloud, and they will likely stumble on the second sentence. Whether they realize it or not, they intuitively know that something is wrong.)

A Sentence a Day

run-ons, spelling, verb form

incorrect

Don't let their cuteness fool you; these adorable fluffy puppys and kittys from Dr. Doominskis lab are extreemly deadly and can kill you with just one bite.

correct

Don't let their cuteness fool you; these adorable, fluffy puppies and kitties from Dr. Doominski's lab are extremely deadly and can kill you with just one bite.

notes

Students may see a semicolon and assume it is wrong. It is not. A semicolon can be used to separate two closely related sentences. (Some believe that the semicolon is slowly disappearing. Some newspapers and magazines rarely, if ever, use it.)

"Puppies" and "kitties" follow a rule common in words ending in a consonant and a *y*: change the *y* to *i* and add "es."

"Extremely" is the correct spelling.

Dr. Doominski should be possessive, since the lab "belongs" to him. Therefore, an apostrophe should appear before the *s*.

semicolons, spelling, apostrophes

A Sentence a Day

My brother Leo, spent the hole morning trying to turn the shower stall into a time machine.

My brother Leo spent the whole morning trying to turn the shower stall into a time machine.

There is no need for a comma after "Leo." People often insert a comma between the subject and verb of a sentence. They should not.

"Leo" is a one-word appositive. Commas are usually eliminated around one-word appositives. However, it would not be incorrect to place a comma both before *and* after "Leo."

A "hole" belongs in the ground. "Whole" refers to all of something.

A Sentence a Day

commas,
word choice

"If you don't volunteer to clean up the mess you made during the food fight," said principle lazoria, "You will spend your next 5 lunch periods eating cold oatmeal in The Office."

"If you don't volunteer to clean up the mess you made during the food fight," said Principal Lazoria, "you will spend your next five lunch periods eating cold oatmeal in the office."

"Principal" is the word to use for a school administrator, not "principle." It is not capitalized except when used with the principal's name, as in "Principal Lazoria."

Principal Lazoria really speaks only one sentence. (Well, he probably speaks *a lot* more of them during this incident, but in the item above, he speaks only one.) It is interrupted with "said Principal Lazoria." Therefore, the second part of the quotation should not be capitalized.

Numbers smaller than ten should be spelled out, not written as numerals.

There is no need to capitalize "the office," unless perhaps you're speaking of the television show by the same name.

word choice, capitalization, spelling

A Sentence a Day

On the campain trail, the excentric politician wore a santa suit and handed out green beens, little packets of catsup, and money tied with brightly, colored ribon.

On the campaign trail, the eccentric politician wore a Santa suit and handed out green beans, little packets of catsup(,) and money tied with brightly colored ribbon.

When it comes to spelling, "campaign" is a doozy of a word. It's a wonder anyone ever gets it right. "Eccentric" isn't easy, either, since it really sounds like it *should* have an *x*. "Beans" and "ribbon" are much easier.

"Santa" should be capitalized because it's a name.

There is no reason to put a comma between "brightly" and "colored." (One test: try putting "and" between the words—"brightly" *and* "colored ribbon." If "and" doesn't sound right, a comma isn't needed.)

A Sentence a Day

spelling, capitalization,
commas

Mr. Pennybroke turned to his son and asked "Remember that new video game you want me to buy for you, the one that is so charmingly titled Do You Want to Harass Your Parents."

Mr. Pennybroke turned to his son and asked, "Remember that new video game you want me to buy for you, the one that is so charmingly titled 'Do You Want to Harass Your Parents?'?"

Correcting this one takes some real care with details. First, a comma must separate Mr. Pennybroke's actual words from the introductory part of the sentence. Therefore, a comma should follow "said."

"Do You Want to Harass Your Parents?" should have quotation marks around it because it is a title. However, because it occurs in a quotation that already *has* quotation marks, the quotation marks should be single.

The video's title itself is a question, so a question mark should be placed inside the single quotes. However, the whole sentence Mr. Pennybroke speaks is also a question. That means a question mark also goes at the end of the sentence. (Yes, it looks very strange. If students get this right, they surely deserve a pat on the back.)

Miss Glenflinkenhaven does two strange things, she insisted on wearing a giant hat made of fruit when she goes grocery shopping, and she plays the harp with her tows.

Miss Glenflinkenhaven does two strange things: she insists on wearing a giant hat made of fruit when she goes grocery shopping, and she plays the harp with her toes.

"Miss Glenflinkenhaven does two strange things" should be followed by a colon. The colon means "Note what follows." (A dash would also be acceptable.)

The entire sentence moves back and forth between present and past tense. It starts out in present tense, so it should continue in present tense.

"Toes" are those appendages on our feet—and also on Miss Glenflinkenhaven's.

A Sentence a Day

123

colons, verb tense, word choice

Never hug a hibble, in a hibble habble horper, never kiss a kibble, in a kibble kabble korper.

Never hug a hibble in a hibble habble horper, and never kiss a kibble in a kibble kabble korper.

Okay, the sentence makes no sense unless you know what a hibble habble horper or a kibble kabble korper is. However, even with such nonsensical words, we can tell that the sentence is a run-on. Two sentences cannot be separated by a comma alone, and it's easy to tell that the item is really two sentences, even if no one has ever even *thought* of hugging a hibble.

There is no need for the commas after "hibble" and "kibble."

run-ons,
commas

A Sentence a Day

Irregardless of your opinion, you have to go to aunt ethels doily crocheting party next Week on Tuesday.

Regardless of your opinion, you have to go to Aunt Ethel's doily crocheting party next week on Tuesday.

"Irregardless" may be in the dictionary, along with "ain't," but it is noted as "non-standard." "Regardless" is the word to use.

Aunt Ethel should be capitalized because it is being used as her name.

An apostrophe should be placed before the *s* in "Aunt Ethel's" to show possession. The doily crocheting party "belongs" to Aunt Ethel.

The word "week" is not capitalized, but names of days of the week are.

A Sentence a Day

word choice, capitalization, apostrophes

Hey, man!
   The college you are president of sounds like really cool and all that and I'd like really like to you know get into it and like find a career that's all about success.

Dear President Malloy:
   I would like to apply to your college to pursue a career in rocket science.

Slang has its place. We all use it. However, we should all know when it's appropriate and when it is not. A college application is not the place for it. The sentence needs to be rewritten.

In addition, it is not a good idea to assume the president is a man. Taking time to find out the president's name is much smarter.

A colon follows the salutation in a business or formal letter.

word choice,
colons

A Sentence a Day

My mom, she worries alot about bed bugs and nuclear war.

My mom worries a lot about bed bugs and nuclear war.

"My mom, she" is a double subject. There is no need to say "she."

"A lot" is two words.

A Sentence a Day

double subjects,
spelling

Blake wanted ice cream. And so the babysitter gave him some. And then she tried to get him to eat carrots, but he wouldn't. And so she poured some choclate syrup on them. And then he did.

Blake wanted ice cream, so the babysitter gave him some. Then she tried to get him to eat carrots, but he wouldn't, so she poured some chocolate syrup on them. Then he did.

There are other ways to "fix" the item above. The problem is the choppiness of all those sentences starting with "and so" and "and then."

"Chocolate" is the correct spelling.

Blake's babysitter is obviously a seasoned professional.

miscellaneous, spelling

A Sentence a Day

Patrice lead the lead pencil boycott because he was a good leeder

Patrice led the lead pencil boycott because he was a good leader.

"Lead" and "led" are often confused, and it's no wonder. "Lead," pronounced to rhyme with "head," is a kind of metal. However, another word that *sounds* the same is "led," which is the past tense of the verb "lead" (pronounced "leed"), as in, "You can lead a horse to water, but you can't make him drink."

A simpler way to think of it: the spelling "led" is used for only one thing—the past tense of the verb "lead," as in, "He led them into battle."

The sentence should end in a period.

A Sentence a Day

word choice, spelling
punctuation

Pickles my "orange tabby cat" clawed her way through the new screen door to chase a couple a robins who weren't at all eager to be somebodys dinner.

Pickles, my orange tabby cat, clawed her way through the new screen door to chase a couple of robins who weren't at all eager to be somebody's dinner.

There is a sad trend in quotation marks. They are appearing everywhere, for no good reason. Restaurants advertise spinach salad with "feta" cheese. Clothing stores advertise new shipments of "turtlenecks." Such quotation marks are completely unnecessary, as are the quotation marks around "orange tabby cat."

"My orange tabby cat" is an appositive that interrupts the sentence to give more information about Pickles. It should be set off with commas.

The phrase "couple of" may sound like "couple a" when we say it, but that's not the way it is spelled.

"Somebody" needs an apostrophe after it to show possession. It's a dinner that "belongs" to somebody.

Harrison looked at his father and goes, "Yuk! Dad why do you always have to ware those plaid golf pants when my friends are around."

Harrison looked at his father and said, "Yuk! Dad, why do you always have to wear those plaid golf pants when my friends are around?"

People "say," not "go." Harrison looked at his father and "said."

Harrison is directly addressing Dad, so "Dad" needs a comma after it.

Harrison is also asking Dad a question. Therefore, a question mark goes after his question, inside the quotation marks.

"Wear" is the correct spelling.

A Sentence a Day

word choice, commas, question marks, spelling

No it's not O.K. with us if your little sister & her friends want to go thru our haunted house with a flashlite because there afraid of the dark.

No, it's not okay with us if your little sister and her friends want to go through our haunted house with a flashlight because they're afraid of the dark.

Introductory words like "yes," "no," "well," and "oh" are followed by a comma.

In all except the most informal writing, "okay" and "and" should be spelled out.

Although "thru" and "lite" are starting to appear everywhere, the correct spellings are "through" and "light." "Flashlight" follows the same principle.

"They're" is the correct spelling of the contraction for "they are."

commas,
spelling

A Sentence a Day

Erin didn't do good on the grammer test.

Erin didn't do well on the grammar test.

To describe how someone *did* something, "well" is the word to use, not "good."

"Grammar" ends in "ar," not "er."

A Sentence a Day

word choice,
spelling

"There isn't nothing you can do to fix that busted lamp," said Jenna to her little brother. "You might as well leave home now.

"There isn't anything you can do to fix that broken lamp," said Jenna to her little brother. "You might as well leave home now."

Double negatives are not a good thing. Jenna should be saying, "There isn't anything you can do…"

"Busted" is considered slang. "Broken" is preferred.

Quotation marks are needed after "now." Quotation marks come in pairs.

If students argue that a direct quotation should quote people accurately, even if they are using double negatives and slang, they are correct. If we assume that Jenna is being quoted accurately, nothing is wrong with the item, except for the missing quotation marks at the end.

double negatives, word choice,
quotation marks

A Sentence a Day

Well him and me gotta go to get some new battries for are automatic pencil washer before we can do are homewrok.

Well, he and I have to go get some new batteries for our automatic pencil washer before we can do our homework.

A comma should be placed after introductory words like "yes," "oh," "no," and "well." However, "well" is often stuck in as a filler and serves no purpose. The sentence would be even more improved if "well" were eliminated altogether.

"Him and me gotta go" should be replaced with "he and I have to go." (A test: rephrase the sentence so that the subject is singular, and see which pronoun sounds right. "Him has to go"? "Me has to go"? No.)

"Batteries" and "homework" are the correct spellings.

"Our" is the word needed, not "are"—even though the spoken "our" often sounds like "are." "Our" is used to show possession.

A Sentence a Day

commas, unnecessary words, pronouns, spelling, word choice while the class takes a test, Mrs. Melktoste is reading an article called how to deal with impossible studnets. It is in the magazine teaching today.

While the class takes a test, Mrs. Melktoste is reading an article called "How to Deal with Impossible Students." It is in the magazine *Teaching Today*.

The sentence should begin with a capital letter.

Titles of magazine articles should be placed in quotation marks. The first, last, and all important words should be capitalized.

"Students" is the correct spelling.

The names of magazines and books are capitalized and placed in italics. (When hand-written, they should be underlined.) However, publications differ in their policies. Some, for example, put magazine titles in quotation marks rather than using italics.

capitalization, quotation marks, spelling, italics

A Sentence a Day

The bigest taco in the entire universe.

Penelope was so hungry she thought she could eat the biggest taco in the entire universe.

The item above is a sentence fragment and can be corrected in many ways. The important thing is that the item needs a verb.

"Biggest" is the correct spelling.

fragments,
spelling

A Sentence a Day

incorrect

"did you remember to write your research paper" asked Mrs. thornwhimple. "oops" said brian.

correct

"Did you remember to write your research paper?" asked Mrs. Thornwhimple.
    "Oops," said Brian.

notes

In dialogue, a new paragraph begins with each change of speakers.

Mrs. Thornwhimple asks a question, so her words should end with a question mark.

Both quotations should begin with capital letters.

"Mrs. Thornwhimple" and "Brian" are proper nouns that should be capitalized.

"Oops" should be separated from the dialogue tag "said Brian" with a comma. (An exclamation point would also be appropriate.)

Witch one is more slower: a turtel with a limp or a groggy snail?

Which one is slower: a turtle with a limp or a groggy snail?

A "witch" rides a broom. "Which" is the word needed here.

The three forms of "slow" are "slow" (to describe one thing), "slower" (to compare two things) and "slowest" (to compare three things.) "More" is unnecessary with "slower."

"Turtle" is the correct spelling.

A good follow-up is to have students try adding to the sentence so that "slowest" is the correct form of the word, as in "Which one is slowest: a turtle with a limp, a groggy snail, or the clock during last period of the school day?"

A Sentence a Day

word choice, unnecessary words
spelling

The family canceled the trip to the beach due to the fact that fish was raining from the sky.

The family canceled the trip to the beach because fish were raining from the sky.

A singular noun pairs with "was." A plural noun pairs with "were." Because "fish" is plural, the verb to use with it is "were."

"Due to the fact that" is not really wrong, but it is a cumbersome phrase. "Because" works much better.

verb form,
unnecessary words

A Sentence a Day

The new teachers plan was based on her beleif that kids' really love to do grammer exercises in english class.

The new teacher's plan was based on her belief that kids really love to do grammar exercises in English class.

The plan "belongs" to the teacher. Therefore, "teacher's" needs an apostrophe before the *s*. (If the plan belonged to a lot of teachers, the apostrophe would go after the *s*.)

"Belief" follows the "*i* before *e* except after *c*" rule.

"Kids" is not a possessive and should not have an apostrophe.

"English" should be capitalized because it is the name of a language.

"Grammar" ends in "ar," not "er."

A Sentence a Day

apostrophes, spelling,
capitalization

When the band started playing a polka at the barnyard wedding all the foul in attendence did the chicken dance.

When the band started playing a polka at the barnyard wedding, all the fowl in attendance did the chicken dance.

"When the band started playing a polka at the barnyard wedding" is an introductory element (a clause) that should be followed by a comma.

"Foul" describes a smell. "Fowl" is used to refer to chickens. (The fowl could smell foul, of course.)

There is a "dance" in the word "attendance."

commas, word choice, spelling

142

A Sentence a Day

Mrs. Elmwood wondered why the dog was green and hairless after it came out of her sons bedroom, but she new that it wasn't her darling littel charlies fault cuz he never told a lie or did anything rong.

Mrs. Elmwood wondered why the dog was green and hairless after it came out of her son's bedroom, but she knew that it wasn't her darling little Charlie's fault because he never told a lie or did anything wrong.

There are two possessives in the sentence: *son's* bedroom and *Charlie's* fault.

"New" might describe the dog's look, but "knew" is the word needed after "she."

"Little," "because," and "wrong" are the correct spellings of the words needed in the last part of the sentence.

A Sentence a Day

apostrophes, word choice, spelling

I couldn't hardly see the rode cuz it was raining cats and dogs.

correct

I could hardly see the road because it was raining cats and dogs.

notes

"Could hardly" is the correct phrase, not "couldn't hardly." ("Couldn't hardly" is considered a double negative.)

"Road" is the word needed here. "Rode" is the past tense of "ride."

"Because" is the correct spelling.

To improve the sentence even further, students might try to eliminate the cliché, "raining cats and dogs." See if they can come up with more original ways to describe how hard it was raining.

double negatives, word choice, spelling

A Sentence a Day

David was furious because he didn't no where his lobster costume was at.

David was furious because he didn't know where his lobster costume was.

"Know" is the word needed, not "no."

"At" is an unnecessary preposition at the end of the sentence.

A Sentence a Day

word choice,
unnecessary words

Because he didn't want to eat his desert in the desert.

Because he didn't want to eat his dessert in the desert, Aaron decided to put his butterscotch pudding in the cooler.

"Dessert" is a sweet something at the end of a meal. A "desert" is a hot and dry place.

The item is a sentence fragment. A good follow-up exercise is to have students correct the fragment in at least five different ways, with "because" in the middle of the sentence as well as at the beginning of the sentence.

Duffy literally jumped out of his skin when he heard the door to his room open at midnight.

Duffy jumped out of his skin when he heard the door to his room open at midnight.

If Duffy *literally* jumped out of his skin, he would be a skeleton. There is an odd trend to use "literally" in a way that makes no sense. "Literally" means "actually." Did Duffy *actually* jump out of his skin? Probably not.

"Jumped out of his skin" is a cliché. The sentence would be improved even further if rewritten to describe Duffy's fear in a fresh, new way. A good follow-up activity is to have students try describing his fear without using "jumped out of his skin."

A Sentence a Day

word choice,
miscellaneous

I'm tired of setting hear, and I hope this boring class will soon be over with so I can excape," exclaimed Seneca!

"I'm tired of sitting here, and I hope this boring class will soon be over so I can escape!" exclaimed Seneca.

People "sit." They "set" things down on tables.

"Hear" is what our ears do. "Here" is where Seneca is sitting.

The word is "escape," not "excape."

Quotation marks come in pairs. They are needed at the beginning and end of a quotation.

There is no need for "with" after the word "over."

In a quotation, the exclamation point goes after the sentence that is an exclamation—and before the quotation marks.

word choice, spelling,
unnecessary words, punctuation

A Sentence a Day

Curled up in his underwear drawer, Abel saw that his new kitten had finally settled down.

Curled up in his underwear drawer, Abel's new kitten had finally settled down.

Dangling modifiers can be unintentionally funny. Abel, of course, is not curled up in his underwear drawer. The cat is. "Curled up in his underwear drawer" must refer to the next noun in the sentence, so that noun should be "kitten," not Abel. (In the incorrect version, "Abel" is a noun. In the correct version, "Abel's" is an adjective describing the noun "kitten.")

A Sentence a Day

dangling modifiers

The squirrel scampered into the house, jumped on the table, and landed on are Thanksgiving Turkey.

The squirrel scampered into the house, jumped on the table, and landed on our Thanksgiving turkey.

Students often mistake "are" for "our," probably because many pronounce the words almost identically.

"Thanksgiving" should be capitalized because it is the name of a holiday. "Turkey" should not be capitalized just because it follows "Thanksgiving."

word choice,
capitalization

A Sentence a Day

Laughing loudly at Earl's joke, the green Jello flew into the air when Gavin tripped.

Laughing loudly at Earl's joke, Gavin tripped and sent green Jello flying into the air.

There are many ways to correct this sentence, which has Jello laughing loudly—an unlikely occurrence. "Laughing loudly at Earl's joke" is a dangling modifier. As written, it describes Jello. The sentence must be rewritten so that it describes "Gavin," the one who really did the laughing.

"Jello" is capitalized because it is a brand name.

A Sentence a Day

dangling modifiers, capitalization

When the hostess told the boys they would have to put on shoes before they could be seated in the restraunt.

When the hostess told the boys they would have to put on shoes before they could be seated in the restaurant, they decided to walk down the street and grab hot dogs from the hot dog cart.

The item above is a fragment and needs to be completed. What happened when the hostess told the boys they would have to put on shoes? A good follow-up activity is to have the students try to complete the sentence at least three different ways.

"Restaurant" is the proper spelling for this difficult word.

fragments,
spelling

A Sentence a Day

The people at the costume party, they complimented one another on their hideously, ugly masks as they enjoyed ordervs made of bat wings and frog eyeballs.

The people at the costume party complimented one another on their hideously ugly masks as they enjoyed hors d'oeuvres made of bat wings and frog eyeballs.

"The people at the costume party" and "they" are the same thing. There is no need for a double subject here. "They" should be omitted.

A test to check if there should be a comma between "hideously" and "ugly" is to try saying "and" between the two words. If "and" works, a comma is needed. In this case, "hideously and ugly masks" does not sound right.

Does anyone really know how to spell "hors d'oeuvres"? Challenge your students to master this very, very difficult word.

double subjects, commas, spelling

incorrect

Rick wouldn't be quite when the teacher said he was waisting the hole class period text messaging his freinds, about the hamster he had one in a radio contest.

correct

Rick wouldn't be quiet when the teacher said he was wasting the whole class period text messaging his friends about the hamster he had won in a radio contest.

notes

The item above is a mess of incorrect word choices and spelling errors. After the students have corrected the sentence, challenge them to write a new sentence using "quite," "waist," "hole," and "one" correctly.

There is no need for a comma after "friends."

word choice, spelling,
commas

A Sentence a Day

When her Dad asked her, "why she came home so late," Mindy studdered, "well my friends and I went to…uh…bible study… and…uh…I guess we lost track of time."

When her dad asked her why she came home so late, Mindy stuttered, "Well, my friends and I went to… uh…Bible study…and…uh…I guess we lost track of time."

In this case, "dad" should not be capitalized because "her" is used with it. In other words, "dad" is not being used as a noun of direct address.

The first part of the sentence is an indirect quotation and does not need quotation marks. "Why she came home so late" are *not* the words that came out of Mindy's dad's mouth.

"Stuttered" has double *t*'s, not double *d*'s.

Introductory words like "yes," "no," "oh," and "well" should be followed by commas.

"Bible" is the name of a book and should be capitalized.

A Sentence a Day

capitalization, quotation marks, spelling, commas

Please tell me that singing this peace of paper will cancel further deliverys of these garden gnomes, which I never ordered, I also never ordered the bags of elephant manure.

Please tell me that signing this piece of paper will cancel further deliveries of these garden gnomes, which I never ordered. I also never ordered the bags of elephant manure.

There is a big difference between "singing" and "signing," just as there is a big difference between "piece" and "peace."

The plural of many words that end in a consonant and *y* is formed by changing the *y* to *i* and adding "es."

The item is a run-on sentence. Two sentences cannot be separated by a comma. A period is needed after the first "ordered."

spelling,
run-ons

A Sentence a Day

Nekita didn't care that she wasn't chosen to go to hollywood after her audition for American Idol, she didn't want to go anyways.

Nekita didn't care that she wasn't chosen to go to Hollywood after her audition for *American Idol*. She didn't want to go anyway.

"Hollywood" is capitalized because it is the name of a certain city.

As the title of a television show, *American Idol* should be italicized or underlined. (Some sources recommend using quotation marks instead of italics for television show titles.)

The correct term is "anyway," not "anyways."

A Sentence a Day

capitalization, italics, word choice

After thinking it over carefully Verna decided she did'nt want either rasberry sauce or choclate sirup on her macaroni and cheese.

After thinking it over carefully, Verna decided she didn't want either raspberry sauce or chocolate syrup on her macaroni and cheese.

"After thinking it over carefully" is an introductory element (a phrase). It should be followed by a comma.

The apostrophe in "didn't" goes between the *n* and the *t*.

"Raspberry," to the surprise of many, has a *p* in it.

"Chocolate" has two *o*'s.

"Syrup" has a *y*, not an *i*.

Because the sun was in my eyes I didn't see the pothole in the road so I hit it with my front tire and flipped over my handle bars and then landed with my face firmly planted on the asphalt and I felt really stupid besides that my face hurt.

Because the sun was in my eyes, I didn't see the pothole in the road. I hit it with my front tire and flipped over my handlebars, landing with my face firmly planted on the asphalt. I felt really stupid. Besides that, my face hurt.

There are a number of ways to fix this run-on sentence. Above is one example.

"Handlebars" is one word.

A Sentence a Day

run-ons,
spelling

I wish I had never went to the party, witch was a nightmair, alot of people who were their got food poisoning from Hannas home made cucumber dip.

I wish I had never gone to the party, which was a nightmare. A lot of people who were there got food poisoning from Hanna's homemade cucumber dip.

"Went" should never be used with a helping verb. "Gone" is the word needed after "had."

"Which," "nightmare," "a lot," and "homemade" are the correct spellings needed.

The sentence is a run-on. A period is needed after "nightmare." There are other possibilities, too, such as eliminating the comma after "nightmare" and adding "because."

"Hanna's" should have an apostrophe since it is a possessive. The dip "belongs" to her.

verb form, spelling,
run-ons, apostrophes

A Sentence a Day

It looked like someone sent a bunch of banana's through a blender and then through the whole thing on top of the toyota.

It looked like someone sent a bunch of bananas through a blender and then threw the whole thing on top of the Toyota.

"Bananas" does not need an apostrophe. The bananas don't possess anything.

"Threw" is the spelling needed when something is tossed.

"Toyota" should be capitalized because it is a car's brand name.

A Sentence a Day

apostrophes, word choice, capitalization

If you sit at you're computer two much. You might turn into a mouse potato.

If you sit at your computer too much, you might turn into a mouse potato.

"Your" is the word needed, not "you're."

"Too" is the word needed, not "two."

The first "sentence" is a fragment. It is really an introductory element (a clause) that should be part of the next sentence.

spelling, fragments

A Sentence a Day

Are Science class with Mr Fentiman is so boaring, my Math class would be boaring, two, but are teacher is miss fazio and she is so beutaful that I don't mind math at all.

Our science class with Mr. Fentiman is so boring. My math class would be boring, too, but our teacher is Miss Fazio, and she is so beautiful that I don't mind math at all.

"Are" should be "our." "Boaring" should be "boring." "Beutaful" should be "beautiful."

"Two" should be "too" because it is used in the sense of "also."

"Mr." needs a period. (It's an abbreviation for "mister.")

"Science" and "math" should not be capitalized. The only school subjects capitalized are languages (English, French) or specific course names (Introduction to Algebra).

A Sentence a Day

word choice, spelling, abbreviations, capitalization

My leg fell a sleep when I was sitting on the grass waiting for Mom to finish talking to my teacher, and Hank Steel, the best looking guy in the world, motions for me to sit next to him on the bleachers, I try to stand up I fell flat on my face.

My leg fell asleep when I was sitting on the grass waiting for Mom to finish talking to my teacher, and Hank Steel, the best looking guy in the world, motioned for me to sit next to him on the bleachers. I tried to stand up and fell flat on my face.

"Asleep" is one word, not two.

The item switches back and forth between past and present tense. Since it starts out in past tense ("leg *fell* asleep"), it should stay in past tense. "Motions" should be "motioned" and "try" should be "tried."

The sentence is also a run-on. The comma after "bleachers" should be a period.

spelling, verb tense,
run-ons

A Sentence a Day

When the toilet made a wierd gurgling sound while I dried my hands, I thought to myself, "please let me get out before it blows" when I left, I herd a enormus explosion.

When the toilet made a weird gurgling sound while I dried my hands, I thought to myself, "Please let me get out before it blows." When I left, I heard an enormous explosion.

"Please" should be capitalized since it is the first word of the sentence in the quotation.

The sentence is a run-on. A period is needed before "when."

"Herd" refers to cattle, not what a person does with ears. The correct spelling here is "heard."

"An" is used before words beginning with a vowel, as in "an enormous explosion."

"Enormous" and "weird" are the correct spellings.

A Sentence a Day

capitalization, run-ons, word choice, spelling

I wonder if elephants have any rythim?

I wonder if elephants have any rhythm.

"Rhythm" is the correct spelling. In this case, *y* is used as a vowel.

The sentence is not a question. It is a statement. A question would be, "Do you ever wonder if elephants have any rhythm?" or "Do elephants have any rhythm?"

spelling,
miscellaneous

A Sentence a Day

My Dentist says that I'm going to loose my teeth if I don't start flossing I wonder if theres such a thing as choclate Dental floss.

My dentist says that I'm going to lose my teeth if I don't start flossing. I wonder if there's such a thing as chocolate dental floss.

"Dentist" should not be capitalized. There is no reason to capitalize "dental," either.

"Lose" is the correct spelling. (If she doesn't floss, however, she might get a *loose* tooth.)

The item is a run-on sentence. A period is needed after "flossing."

"There's" should have an apostrophe before the *s*. It is a contraction of "there is."

There are two *o*'s in "chocolate."

A Sentence a Day

capitalization, spelling, run-ons

incorrect

If we have to eat Tuna casserole one more night for dinner. I'm going to screem.

correct

If we have to eat tuna casserole one more night for dinner, I'm going to scream.

notes

"Tuna" should not be capitalized.

"If we have to eat tuna casserole one more night for dinner" is a fragment. It should be part of the next sentence, separated by a comma.

"Scream" is the correct spelling for what someone does after eating tuna casserole for too many nights straight.

capitalization, fragments,
spelling

A Sentence a Day

Benny our nieghbor that likes to get up at 5 evry saturday morning to mow the lawn and drive all the nieghbors crazy.

Benny, our neighbor who likes to get up at 5:00 every Saturday morning to mow the lawn and drive all the neighbors crazy, is not the most popular guy on our block.

The item above is a fragment. Everything that follows "Benny" is part of a long appositive giving more information about "Benny." After the appositive, the sentence needs to be completed.

"Who" refers to people, and "that" refers to things.

The time should be written as "5:00."

"Every" and "neighbors" are the correct spellings.

Names of days of the week are capitalized.

A Sentence a Day

fragments, word choice, spelling, capitalization

Paula was so proud of her newest invenshun a glow-in-the-dark plunger.

Paula was so proud of her newest invention: a glow-in-the-dark plunger.

"Invention" is the correct spelling.

The first part of the sentence "announces" something—a perfect opportunity for a colon. A dash would also work, and so would a comma.

spelling,
colons

A Sentence a Day

Steves' stomach reminded him that judgeing the chili cook-off, and participating in the catamaran race, on the same day, was not a good plan.

Steve's stomach reminded him that judging the chili cook-off and participating in the catamaran race on the same day was not a good plan.

"Steve's" should have an apostrophe before the *s*, not after. (Putting it after the *s* would indicate more than one Steve.)

"Judging" has no *e*. Many words drop the final *e* when adding "ing."

The writer has gone a bit comma crazy on this one. Actually, no commas at all are necessary.

A Sentence a Day

apostrophes, spelling, commas

Sometimes you have to do things you don't want to do, the father reminded his son as they put on candy cane hats and waited for their cue to appeer on stage.

"Sometimes you have to do things you don't want to do," the father reminded his son as they put on candy cane hats and waited for their cue to appear on stage.

Because the father's exact words are used, they should be enclosed in quotation marks.

"Appear" is the correct spelling.

A comma is acceptable after "sometimes," though it isn't necessary.

quotation marks,
spelling

A Sentence a Day

Flora smiled, and introduced her too hanging plants as Phil and Rhoda Dendron.

Flora smiled and introduced her two hanging plants as Phil and Rhoda Dendron.

There is no need to use a comma between the two parts of a compound verb (smiled and introduced).

"Two" is the word to use when expressing a number.

A Sentence a Day

commas,
spelling

Who *does* like green eggs and ham, I sertainly do'nt, I do'n't even like green things that are *suppose* to be green.

Who *does* like green eggs and ham? I certainly don't. I don't even like green things that are *supposed* to be green.

The item is a run-on sentence. The first part is a question and needs a question mark. A period is needed after "I certainly don't."

"Certainly" is the correct spelling.

"Don't" is the correct spelling. The apostrophe goes between the *n* and the *t*, to represent the *o* that is left out of "not."

Though it may sound like "suppose to" when someone says it, the phrase is really "supposed to," with a *d*.

run-ons, spelling,
apostrophes

A Sentence a Day

Diegos dream was to launch his special paper airplane from the top of the eiffel tower in paris. Or at least from the top of duke's plumbing supply in paris, texas.

Diego's dream was to launch his special paper airplane from the top of the Eiffel Tower in Paris, or at least from the top of Duke's Plumbing Supply in Paris, Texas.

The dream "belongs" to Diego. Therefore, "Diego's" is possessive and needs an apostrophe.

"Eiffel Tower" is the name of a certain structure, so it is capitalized, as is "Paris," the name of a city.

Duke's Plumbing Supply is the name of a store, so it should be capitalized.

"Or at least from the top of Duke's Plumbing Supply" is a sentence fragment. It should be part of the previous sentence, separated by a comma or a dash.

A Sentence a Day

apostrophes, capitalization, fragments

Because the students names came over the intercom in a voice that definately didn't sound very happy.

Because the students' names came over the intercom in a voice that definitely didn't sound very happy, the students weren't exactly eager to report to the office.

The names belong to more than one student. Therefore, the apostrophe goes *after* the *s*.

The item is a sentence fragment that needs to be completed.

"Definitely" definitely does not have an *a* in it.

apostrophes, fragments, spelling

A Sentence a Day

The classroom hamster was a fussy little thing, the students' tried to feed it lettuce but it wouldn't eat anything except chunks of leftover bean burritoes.

The classroom hamster was a fussy little thing. The students tried to feed it lettuce, but it wouldn't eat anything except chunks of leftover bean burritos.

Because "students" is not a possessive here, it needs no apostrophe.

The item is a run-on sentence. A comma cannot be used, by itself, to separate two sentences, so a period (or a semicolon) is needed after "thing."

A comma is needed after lettuce since "The students tried to feed it lettuce, but it wouldn't eat anything except chunks of bean burritos" is a compound sentence. A compound sentence requires a comma along with a coordinating conjunction ("and," "but," "or," "for, " "nor," "yet," "so").

There is no *e* in "burritos."

A Sentence a Day

apostrophes, run-ons, spelling

Dee desided to quit her job at dottie's dairy delight because the double chocolate mocha malts were delighting her a little to much, she had gained ten lbs. since starting the job only a Month ago.

Dee decided to quit her job at Dottie's Dairy Delight because the double chocolate mocha malts were delighting her a little too much. She had gained ten pounds since starting the job only a month ago.

"Decided" has no *s* in it.

"Dottie's Dairy Delight" should be capitalized because it is the name of a certain store.

The malts delighted Dee "too" much. "Too" is used to mean "very."

Except in very informal writing or in lists, "pounds" should be written out, not abbreviated as "lbs."

Names of months are capitalized, but the word "month" is not.

The comma between "much" and "she" should be replaced with a period in order to eliminate a run-on sentence.

spelling, capitalization, word choice
abbreviations, run-ons

A Sentence a Day

Balancing a birthday cake with flaming candles on his head Travis was the life some would say "light" of the party.

Balancing a birthday cake with flaming candles on his head, Travis was the life—some would say "light"—of the party.

"Balancing a birthday cake with flaming candles on his head" is an introductory element (a phrase). It should be followed by a comma.

"Some would say 'light'" is an aside, an interruption. It should be set off with dashes or put in parentheses.

A Sentence a Day

*commas,
miscellaneous*

Frank a chimpanzee was totaly in love with gladys a aardvark.

Frank, a chimpanzee, was totally in love with Gladys, an aardvark.

The sentence contains two appositives that should be set off with commas: "a chimpanzee" and "an aardvark."

"Totally" has two *l*'s.

"Gladys" is capitalized because it is a proper noun.

"An" is used before words that begin with a vowel sound.

commas, spelling,
capitalization, word choice

A Sentence a Day

The alien the one who had traveled 27 light-years to reach the earth was dissapointed to find that the coffee shop hed had his eye on for 20 light-years was out of expresso.

The alien, the one who had traveled 27 light-years to reach the earth, was disappointed to find that the coffee shop he'd had his eye on for 20 light-years was out of espresso.

"The one who had traveled 27 light-years to reach the earth" is an interrupting element (an appositive) that should be set off with commas.

"Disappointed" has one *s* and two *p*'s.

Though many people pronounce it "expresso," the word is really "espresso." With Starbucks so rapidly proliferating all over the country, perhaps "espresso" should be a required spelling word these days.

"He'd" is a contraction of "he had" and requires an apostrophe.

A Sentence a Day

commas, spelling, apostrophes

"When you say your going to die if you have to go to school on a bair hair day I think your exaggerating just a bit" said Jennifers mother.

"When you say you're going to die if you have to go to school on a bad hair day, I think you're exaggerating just a bit," said Jennifer's mother.

"You're" is the correct word to use when "you are" can be substituted in the sentence.

"When you say you're going to die if you have to go to school on a bad hair day" is an introductory element (a clause). It should be separated from the rest of the sentence with a comma.

There should be a comma after "bit," to separate the words in the direct quotation from the dialogue tag, "said Jennifer's mother."

The mother "belongs" to Jennifer. "Jennifer's" needs an apostrophe to show possession.

word choice, commas,
apostrophes

A Sentence a Day

Orin's grandmother just couldn't beleive he didn't like cute stuffed bears alphabet blocks and his tricycle anymore, even though he was about to graduate from high school.

Orin's grandmother just couldn't believe he didn't like cute stuffed bears, alphabet blocks(,) and his tricycle anymore, even though he was about to graduate from high school.

Items in a series should be separated by commas. The comma before "or" is optional.

"Believe" follows the "*i* before *e* except after *c*" rule.

A Sentence a Day

commas,
spelling

Casey likes new england clam chowder, but his dad, he prefers manhattan clam chowder, his sister, though, gets nauseous even thinking about clam chowder.

Casey likes New England clam chowder, but his dad prefers Manhattan clam chowder. His sister, though, gets nauseous even thinking about clam chowder.

"New England" and "Manhattan" are capitalized because they are the names of specific places.

"His dad, he" is a double subject. There is no need for the "he" or the comma after "dad."

The item is a run-on sentence. A period should replace the comma after "Manhattan clam chowder."

capitalization, double subjects, run-ons

A Sentence a Day

Isadora looked at the picture of prairie chickens in her science book and wondered, "are there also forest chickens, swamp chickens, and mountain chickens.

Isadora looked at the picture of prairie chickens in her science book and wondered, "Are there also forest chickens, swamp chickens(,) and mountain chickens?"

The first word of a sentence in a quotation should be capitalized. Therefore, "are" should be capitalized.

The sentence in quotation marks is a question, so it should end in a question mark.

Quotation marks always come in pairs. They occur at the beginning *and* at the end of a quotation.

Items in a series should be separated by commas. The comma before "and" is optional.

A Sentence a Day

capitalization, question marks,
quotation marks, commas

Henry looked at his grown son sighed and said, do you have any life goals besides trying to acquire the largest television set known to humankind?

Henry looked at his grown son, sighed(,) and said, "Do you have any life goals besides trying to acquire the largest television set known to humankind?"

Items in a series should be separated by commas. The comma before the final "and" is optional.

A direct quotation should be enclosed in quotation marks.

The first word of a sentence in a quotation should be capitalized.

commas, quotation marks, capitalization

A Sentence a Day

Jeremiah glared at the girls laughing at him. "Well *you* try riding a bicicle while you're wearing giant plastic duck feet" he yelled!

Jeremiah glared at the girls laughing at him. "Well, *you* try riding a bicycle while you're wearing giant plastic duck feet!" he yelled.

Introductory words like "yes," "no," "oh," and "well" should be followed by a comma.

"Bicycle" has only one *i*.

The exclamation point belongs after Jeremiah's words, not after "he yelled."

A Sentence a Day

commas, spelling, punctuation

Madeline didn't like the spam that came with her e-mail, the spam that her grandma always fried up with eggs in the morning, or spamalot, the Broadway musical.

Madeline didn't like the spam that came with her e-mail, the Spam that her grandma always fried up with eggs in the morning, or *Spamalot*, the Broadway musical.

"Spam" is used in two different ways. The Spam that comes in a can is capitalized because it is a brand name. The other kind of spam is not.

"Spamalot" is capitalized and italicized because it is the name of a musical.

Items in a series should be separated by commas. The final comma is optional.

capitalization,
commas

A Sentence a Day

Clarissa loves the music of the green electrodes, her mother on the other hand does not.

Clarissa loves the music of the Green Electrodes. Her mother, on the other hand, does not.

The name of the band should be capitalized.

A comma cannot be used to separate two sentences. A period or a semicolon should follow "Green Electrodes."

Parenthetical expressions like "on the other hand," "by the way," and "in my opinion" should be set off with commas.

A Sentence a Day

capitalization, run-ons,
commas

little Salvadors uncle from jackson wyoming told him he was coming to see him and bringing along his favorite moose.

Little Salvador's uncle from Jackson, Wyoming, told him he was coming to see him and bringing along his favorite moose.

"Little" should be capitalized, since it is the beginning of the sentence.

"Salvador's" needs an apostrophe. The uncle "belongs" to Salvador.

"Jackson" and "Wyoming" should be capitalized.

A comma should be place after "Jackson" and after "Wyoming." (Most people remember the comma between the city and state. However, a comma should also be used after the state.)

capitalization, apostrophes,
commas

A Sentence a Day

As the secret hatch slowly creaked open and a blew tentacle uncoiled from the darkness.

As the secret hatch slowly creaked open and a blue tentacle uncoiled from the darkness, Timothy decided it was time to go.

"Blue" is the word to use when referring to a color. "Blew" is what the wind did yesterday.

The item is a sentence fragment that needs to be completed. What happened as the secret hatch opened and the tentacle uncoiled?

A Sentence a Day

word choice,
fragments

Mark stood in front of his teacher, and said "Miss Nordlestorp I know you won't beleive me but my dog ate not only my homework but also my Game Boy and my favorite socks."

Mark stood in front of his teacher and said, "Miss Nordlestorp, I know you won't believe me, but my dog ate not only my homework but also my Game Boy and my best socks."

There is no need for a comma after "teacher." A comma *is* needed after "said."

Mark is directly addressing Miss Nordlestorp, so a comma is needed after her name.

"Believe" follows the "*i* before *e* except after *c*" rule.

"I know you won't believe me, but my dog ate…" is a compound sentence. A comma is used before the coordinating conjunction in a compound sentence. (No comma is needed in "not only my homework but also my Game Boy" because there "but" is not acting as a conjunction separating two complete sentences.)

A Sentence a Day

Learn how to play the kazoo Charlie, or your out of the band.

Learn how to play the kazoo, Charlie, or you're out of the band.

"Charlie" is being directly addressed, so his name should be set off with commas.

"You're" is the word needed.

commas,
word choice

A Sentence a Day

The hover car zoomed across the hot dessert, carrying the accordianists to their sold-out concert in las vegas.

The hover car zoomed across the hot desert, carrying the accordionists to their sold-out concert in Las Vegas.

The accordionists were not, presumably, zooming across a dish of hot apple cobbler. Therefore, the word needed is "desert," not "dessert."

"Accordionists" has only one *a*, the first one. (Perhaps not everyone needs to know that "accordion" doesn't end in "an." What is important is that students know to check the spelling of any word that is the least bit unfamiliar.)

Names of cities should be capitalized.

word choice, spelling,
capitalization

A Sentence a Day

Why would anyone ever want to become a dentist wondered rochelle. I can't imagine spending my life looking at peoples teeth and gums. Me, neither, said Cooper. I'd much rather be a podiatrist and look at peoples feet.

"Why would anyone ever want to become a dentist?" wondered Rochelle. "I can't imagine spending my life looking at people's teeth and gums."

"Me, neither," said Cooper. "I'd much rather be a podiatrist and look at people's feet."

In dialogue, a new paragraph begins with each change of speakers.

A question mark is needed after "Why would anyone ever want to become a dentist?"

Quotation marks should be used around the exact words spoken by a character.

"People's" should have an apostrophe before the *s*. The teeth "belong" to people.

A Sentence a Day

dialogue, question marks,
quotation marks, apostrophes

Little Nathaniel looked up at his angry mother and said, "A rabbit came into my room and said, Don't listen to anything your Mother says. He seemed like a smart rabbit, so I desided to do what he said."

Little Nathaniel looked up at his angry mother and said, "A rabbit came into my room and said, 'Don't listen to anything your mother says.' He seemed like a smart rabbit, so I decided to do what he said."

Neither use of "mother" should be capitalized. "Mother" should be capitalized only when it is used as a person's name.

"Decided" is the correct spelling.

Nathaniel is being quoted, and he in turn is quoting the rabbit. What Nathaniel says should be placed inside double quotation marks. What the rabbit says should be placed inside single quotation marks. (Students may be interested to know that the British do it in exactly the opposite way. They use single quotes around a quotation, with double quotes for a quotation within a quotation.)

capitalization, spelling,
quotation marks

A Sentence a Day

I love hamburgers more than just about anything in the world, except maybe for Emma Sue Taguchi." said Craig. "Hamburgers are alot more loveable than Emma Sue Taguchi in my opinion" said John.

"I love hamburgers more than just about anything else in the world, except maybe for Emma Sue Taguchi," said Craig.

"Hamburgers are a lot more loveable than Emma Sue Taguchi, in my opinion," said John.

In dialogue, a new paragraph begins with each change of speakers.

A comma should separate the quotation from dialogue tags like "he said."

"A lot" is two words, not one.

Parenthetical expressions such as "on the other hand," "as a matter of fact," and "in my opinion" should be set off with commas.

A Sentence a Day

dialogue, spelling, commas

To boys and to grills went two see the amazing poodles play volleyball but they're patients ran out when they had too weight so long for a ticket.

Two boys and two girls went to see the amazing poodles play volleyball, but their patience ran out when they had to wait so long for a ticket.

This sentence is a perfect illustration of the limits of spell-check programs. Spell-check would find nothing wrong with the sentence when, in fact, there are many errors.

Because the sentence is a compound sentence (two complete sentences connected with "but"), a comma is needed before "but." Compound sentences are punctuated with a comma *and* a coordinating conjunction ("and," "but," "or," "for," "nor," "yet," "so.").

spelling, word choice, commas

A Sentence a Day

The frist thing Eric did after he looked out his window and saw the ostrich standing beside the diving bored of the swimming pool.

The first thing Eric did after he looked out his window and saw the ostrich standing beside the diving board of the swimming pool was grab his digital camera and take a picture.

The item is a sentence fragment and needs to be completed. *What* was the first thing Eric did?

"First" is the correct spelling.

The ostrich was standing beside the diving "board," not "bored." (The ostrich might have been "bored," but we don't know that from the sentence.)

A Sentence a Day

fragments, spelling, word choice

My freind visited yesterday and he looks at my room and goes, "Don't you find black walls kinda depressing."

My friend visited yesterday, and he looked at my room and said, "Don't you find black walls kind of depressing?"

"Friend" follows the "*i* before *e* except after *c*" rule.

Because the item is a compound sentence, a comma should be placed before "and."

The sentence starts out in past tense ("visited"), so it should not switch to present tense ("looks").

The friend didn't "go." He "said."

"Kinda" should be written "kind of."

The friend asked a question, so the quotation should end in a question mark.

spelling, commas, verb tense,
word choice, question marks

A Sentence a Day

Egbert use to say he liked eggplant, but then he tasted it, and changed his mind.

Egbert used to say he liked eggplant, but then he tasted it and changed his mind.

"Use to" should be "used to."

There is no need for a comma between compound verbs ("tasted" and "changed").

A Sentence a Day

spelling, miscellaneous

Brad is flying to england in the Fall to visit museums with his Grandmother, but what he is really looking forward to is flying to hawaii next July to serf with his Brother.

Brad is flying to England in the fall to visit museums with his grandmother, but what he is really looking forward to is flying to Hawaii next July to surf with his brother.

"England" and "Hawaii" are the names of specific places, so they should be capitalized.

Months of the year are capitalized, but seasons are not.

"Grandmother" should be capitalized only when it is being used as a person's name, as in, "Will you go with me, Grandmother?"

"Surf" is the word to use for what a person might do in Hawaii. "Serf" refers to a kind of slave.

"Brother" should not be capitalized since it is not a specific name.

capitalization,
word choice

A Sentence a Day

Noone knows why elwood showed up covered in bean dip and looking mad, everyone was afraid to ask, though.

No one knows why Elwood showed up covered in bean dip and looking mad. Everyone was afraid to ask, though.

"No one" is two words.

"Elwood" is a proper noun and should be capitalized.

A comma should not be used to separate two complete sentences. Therefore, a period should replace the comma after "mad."

A Sentence a Day

spelling, capitalization,
run-ons

Where in the world did you put my faverit chicken statue at.

Where in the world did you put my favorite chicken statue?

"Favorite" is the correct spelling.

Because the sentence is a question, it should end in a question mark.

"At" is completely unnecessary at the end of the sentence.

spelling, question marks,
unnecessary words

A Sentence a Day

Miss Edwards the first grade teacher at fernwood elementary school was trying to be kind when she told Chandlers parents that he was a very exuberant child who loved experimenting with language, what she meant was that he was wild and used bad words.

Miss Edwards, the first grade teacher at Fernwood Elementary School, was trying to be kind when she told Chandler's parents that he was a very exuberant child who loved experimenting with language. What she meant was that he was wild and used bad words.

"The first grade teacher at Fernwood Elementary School" is an interrupting element (an appositive) that should be set off with commas.

"Fernwood Elementary School" should be capitalized.

"Chandler's" should have an apostrophe before the *s*. The parents "belong" to Chandler.

The item is a run-on sentence. A period should replace the comma after "language."

"I hate frogs even more than I hate you" exclaimed little Ashley when Charlie presented her with one during reces.

"I hate frogs even more than I hate you!" exclaimed little Ashley when Charlie presented her with one during recess.

Since Ashley "exclaimed," the quotation should have an exclamation point after it.

"Recess" is the correct spelling.

When there knew kitten started scratching olive the furniture, the Peterson family got pretty flustrated and regretted they're decision to get a kitten instead of an aquarium full of fish.

When their new kitten started scratching all of the furniture, the Peterson family got pretty frustrated and regretted their decision to get a kitten instead of an aquarium full of fish.

The sentence has many spelling/word choice errors, all corrected above. Interestingly, many people incorrectly use "flustrated," instead of "frustrated." One theory is that they are confusing "flustered" and "frustrated."

*spelling,
word choice*

INDEX

Errors in the following occur throughout the book and are too numerous to list:
— capitalization
— commas
— spelling
— word choice